# Fruit Desserts

ALSO BY LISA YOCKELSON

*The Efficient Epicure*
*Glorious Gifts from Your Kitchen*
*Country Pies*
*Country Cakes*
*Country Cookies*

# Fruit Desserts

## LISA YOCKELSON

HarperCollins*Publishers*

FIRST EDITION

*Designed by Helene Berinsky*

Library of Congress Cataloging-in-Publication Data

Yockelson, Lisa.
    Fruit desserts/Lisa Yockelson.—1st ed.
        p.   cm.
    Includes index.
    ISBN 0-06-016452-2
    1. Desserts.   2. Cookery (Fruit)   I. Title.
TX773.Y64   1991
641.8′6—dc20                                              90-41731

91 92 93 94 95 CG/RRD 10 9 8 7 6 5 4 3 2 1

*for Susan Friedland,*
*with very special thanks*

# Contents

# Acknowledgments

Baking with fruit (especially pies, tarts, and cakes) and making luxurious fruit compotes and frosty fruit-filled beverages have always been very appealing to me as a cook. Every summer, I join masses of people who, just like me, flock to farms and orchards to gather up the abundance of the season. Sometimes I get together with food-loving friends to make up a batch of chutney or a pot of preserves, and always make time to stock the larder with homemade fruit syrups and fruit vinegars.

The fruit desserts of my childhood—blackberry pie, blueberry cake, lime sherbet, a raspberry-tinged mixed fruit compote—are the delightful sweets that I remember eating every June, July, and August. Now I enjoy making fruit desserts all year round and hope that you, with this book in hand, will find a place for these specialties in your menus, too.

For their talent and professional acumen, I wish to thank the following people:

At HarperCollins, my editor, Susan Friedland, both generated the idea and presided over the manuscript for *Fruit Desserts*, adding her own measure of form and polish to what follows; I am appreciative of her insights into the process of writing and publishing cookbooks. Joseph Montebello, Creative Director, contributed his

share of style to *Fruit Desserts* by taking my collection of recipes and turning them into an appealing book.

At Lescher and Lescher, Ltd., Susan Lescher, my literary agent, works in the world of cookbooks with keen intuition and wisdom and, as always, I value her help. And Carolyn Larson, assistant to Susan Lescher, takes care of business with such elegance.

At La Cuisine in Alexandria, Virginia, proprietress Nancy Pollard seems to share my passion for quality cookware. From her shop I have amassed many lovely pieces of bakeware and oven-to-table dishes into which I have poured, spooned, and, and otherwise arranged many of the desserts in this volume. And at both Williams-Sonoma and Kitchen Bazaar, in Washington, D.C., the managers and staff take pride in sustaining food writers and good cooks alike with their commitment to excellence—from well-chosen pieces of equipment to food products to cookbooks.

At home, many good friends keep me on track, making late-night runs to the market for just one more pound of cherries, cooking dinner for *me*, leaving half-bushel baskets of apples on my doorstep, providing words of encouragement during our telephone chats, and so on. You know who you are. Too, I am most grateful to the many professionals who, over the years, have nurtured, advised, or supported. Among them: Ann Amernick, Patricia Brown, Carol Cutler, Susan Derecskey, Lisa Ekus, Linda Greider, Bob Kelleter, Carol Mason, Phyllis Richman, and Barbara Witt. Many thanks to the ever-patient and skillful Eric Shangold, who helped me become computerized.

And to Steven the Bear, whose favorite fruit dessert is chocolate layer cake.

# Fruit Desserts

# Introduction

## A Revival of Fruit Desserts

Sweet and tart or creamy and suave, desserts made from fresh fruit take full advantage of the abundance of the summer farm stand, autumn harvest, or winter citrus crop. All the splendid sweets—cobblers and shortcake, crisps, puddings, compotes and salads, fools, cakes, tarts, pies, and ice cream—are distinctive because they rely on the natural flavor of the fruit for their savor.

As one season fades into another, a different range of fruit appears in the market, nudging good cooks to compose desserts out of what the land produces. In summer, just seeing piles of peaches, nectarines, plums, and berries persuades us to bake pies and tarts—and dust off the ice cream maker. In the breezy, cooler months of early autumn, apples get baked or sliced for crisps and pies, and pears are readied for poaching, baking, or turning into pies or tarts. During the blustery days of winter, diced and marinated dried fruit appears in compotes and in cake batters; the flavor of orange and grapefruit brightens cakes and compotes, and bananas are treated to a royal grilling with brown sugar and rum. In springtime, strawberries are turned into compotes or served with shortcake, and rhubarb is made into a fruit crisp or compote.

Over the years, hand-picking fruit at local orchards and farms provided much of the inspiration for this book. A bushel or two of apples plucked right from trees grown in Virginia yielded pints and pints of apple butter, a few quarts of applesauce, and fillings for open-faced tarts and turnovers galore. Another time, a load of peaches was processed into peach butter and jam, and quarts of lightly sweetened sliced peaches were frozen for fall and winter consumption. A few loaves of peach bread, several pies, and plate-fuls of shortcake were made out of the ripest fruit that remained.

And one summer day, a friend deposited about ten quarts of wild blueberries on my kitchen counter. These, over the course of a few days, were turned into sauce, frozen both in and out of syrup, stirred into muffin and cake batters, and tossed into a pie shell. Even though I had my fill of berries that summer, I was happy to pull out a bag of frozen berries one snowy winter day and add them to a batch of dough for scones.

Desserts made with fruit have a certain vitality, and the recipes in this collection were created to capture that vigor and, of course, to renew interest in working with fresh fruit. In making these desserts, I'd encourage you to follow nature's own clock, using fruit that's choice and abounding as it appears each season.

# 1

## Compotes and Salads

Berry Compote with Soft and Creamy Vanilla Sauce

Summer Fruit Medley with Meringues

Apricot, Peach, and Nectarine Compote

Melon Compote in Ginger-Lime Syrup

Grapefruit and Orange Compote

Prune Compote

Orange-Stewed Quince

Mélange of Dried Fruit with Cinnamon Crème Fraîche

Rhubarb Compote
Variation: Strawberry-Rhubarb Compote

Strawberries in Red Wine Syrup

Figs in Bourbon-Vanilla Syrup
Variation: Dried Figs in Bourbon-Vanilla Syrup

Figs in Orange Juice

*Strawberries Cardinal*

*Peaches in Sparkling White Wine*

*Applesauce*
Variations: Susan Friedland's Applesauce
Prune-Applesauce, Dried Apricot–Applesauce, Pear-Applesauce,
Fig-Applesauce, Raisin and Date Applesauce

*Summer Berry Bowl*

Compotes and salads made from luscious whole fruit, berries, or a combination of both are really very straightforward to prepare. Most times the fruit is lightly tossed in or briefly cooked with some kind of syrup or sweetener, and served plain or with a sauce. And don't forget that sliced ripe fruit or fresh berries tossed in a few tablespoons of homemade fruit syrup (see pages 170–172 for the method) makes an instant dessert.

A basket of cookies, such as sand dollars, snickerdoodles, or gingersnaps, or a plate of thinly sliced pound cake would complement any of the fruit salads or compotes in this chapter.

*Compotes and Salads*

[5]

# Berry Compote with
# Soft and Creamy Vanilla Sauce

Here, a cascade of vanilla sauce naps a mound of mixed berries—a delightful way to combine fruit and cream. The sauce is really a stirred custard cooked on the top of the stove, cooled, chilled, and lightened by a final fold-through of whipped cream. The sauce can partner almost any kind of fruit compote, crisp, cobbler, or pie.

[SERVES 6]

**For the soft and creamy vanilla sauce:**

*4 extra-large egg yolks, at room temperature*
*2 tablespoons Vanilla-Scented Superfine Sugar (page 173), or plain superfine sugar*
*1½ cups light cream*

*1¼ teaspoons pure vanilla extract*
*⅔ cup cold heavy cream*
*1 tablespoon unsifted confectioners' sugar*

**For the berry compote:**

*2 cups red, ripe raspberries, or golden raspberries*
*2 cups blueberries*
*2 cups blackberries, tossed with 3 tablespoons honey (or more to taste) and left to stand 15 minutes*

*¼ cup crème de cassis (black currant liqueur)*
*6 sprigs fresh mint (optional)*

For the vanilla sauce, beat the egg yolks and superfine sugar in a heavy medium-sized saucepan (preferably enameled cast iron) until thick, about 2 minutes. Whisk the light cream into the egg yolks. Cook over low heat, stirring constantly with a wooden spoon, until the mixture thickens, coats the back of the spoon,

*Fruit Desserts*

[6]

and registers 175 degrees on a candy thermometer. (If you try to hasten the cooking of the sauce by raising the heat, the egg yolks will curdle.) Remove from the heat and stir for 1 minute. Blend in the vanilla. Strain the sauce through a fine-mesh sieve into a storage container. Press a sheet of plastic wrap directly on the top of the sauce to prevent a skin from forming, cool completely, cover, and refrigerate. Chill the sauce until cold, about 6 hours. (The sauce may be prepared up to this point 2 days in advance.)

To finish the sauce, whip the heavy cream until soft peaks form; blend in the confectioners' sugar. Stir a spoonful of the whipped cream into the custard sauce, then fold in the remaining cream. Refrigerate the sauce while you are preparing the berries.

For the berry compote, toss the berries with the cassis in a mixing bowl.

Mound the berries onto 6 deep dessert plates, dividing them evenly among them. Spoon a portion of the sauce over the top of the berries. Tuck a sprig of mint into each pile of berries, if you like, and serve.

*Compotes and Salads*

# Summer Fruit Medley
## with Meringues

Large meringue kisses are a light and crisp counterpoint to a fresh fruit salad.

[SERVES 8]

**For the meringues:**

*2 extra-large egg whites (about ⅓ cup), at room temperature*
*Pinch cream of tartar*

*6 tablespoons plus 1 teaspoon superfine sugar*
*½ teaspoon pure vanilla extract*

**For the fruit medley:**

*3 ripe peaches, peeled, halved, pitted, and sliced*
*3 ripe nectarines, halved, pitted, and sliced*
*3 ripe plums, halved, pitted, and sliced*
*1 cup strawberries, hulled and halved*

*1 cup blueberries, picked over*
*3 tablespoons fruit syrup, homemade (pages 170–172) or store-bought*
*1 tablespoon freshly squeezed lemon juice*
*¾ cup cold heavy cream*

Line a jelly roll pan with a sheet of parchment paper. Set aside. Preheat the oven to 225 degrees.

For the meringues, place the egg whites in a deep bowl and beat until foamy, using a hand-held electric beater. Add the cream of tartar and continue beating until moderately firm peaks are formed. On moderate speed, beat in the 6 tablespoons of sugar, a tablespoon at a time, beating well after each addition. Add the vanilla and beat for 1 minute on high speed. The meringue should be thick, stiff, and glossy. Drop 8 large spoonfuls of the meringue onto the

parchment-lined pan, spacing the mounds about 2½ inches apart. Dust the top of the meringues with the remaining 1 teaspoon sugar.

Bake the meringues on a rack set in the lower third of the preheated oven for about 1 hour and 30 minutes to 1 hour and 50 minutes, or until they are firm, crisp, and dry. Turn off the oven, set the door ajar, and let them stand in the oven for 1 hour.

Transfer the meringues to a cooling rack. Cool for 30 minutes. Peel the meringues from the parchment paper, return them to the cooling rack, and cool completely. The meringues may be used now or stored in an airtight tin for up to 1 week.

For the fruit medley, toss the peaches, nectarines, plums, strawberries, blueberries, fruit syrup, and lemon juice in a large nonreactive bowl. Let stand for 10 minutes.

Whip the cream until soft peaks form.

For each dessert, spoon a helping of fruit onto each large dessert plate, prop a meringue to one side of the fruit, and garnish with a spoonful of the whipped cream. Serve immediately.

## Apricot, Peach, and Nectarine Compote

A light, summery compote that tastes good with crisp vanilla wafers.

[SERVES 6]

1¼ cups white grape juice

2 tablespoons honey, or more to taste, or fresh fruit syrup (pages 170–172)

8 ripe fresh apricots, halved, pitted, and thickly sliced

4 ripe peaches, peeled, halved, pitted, and thickly sliced

3 ripe nectarines, halved, pitted, and thickly sliced

Pour the grape juice into a nonreactive bowl and stir in the honey or fruit syrup. Add the apricots, peaches, and nectarines, and carefully stir through the syrup. Refrigerate for 20 minutes before serving.

## Melon Compote in Ginger-Lime Syrup

Serve this compote all by itself, or with slices of gingerbread or pound cake, or a basket of shortbread.

[SERVES 8]

¼ cup freshly squeezed lime juice

1 teaspoon finely grated lime peel

¼ cup honey

2 tablespoons chopped ginger preserved in syrup

4 cups cubed and seeded watermelon

3 cups cubed cantaloupe

3 cups cubed honeydew melon

2 cups cubed cranshaw melon

12 fresh mint leaves

Mint sprigs (optional)

Blend the lime juice, lime peel, honey, and ginger in a small bowl. Place the melon cubes in a large serving bowl, pour over the honey-lime syrup, scatter over the mint leaves, and toss. (The compote may be made up to 6 hours in advance omitting the mint leaves. Refrigerate in an airtight container. Add the mint leaves just before serving.)

Garnish with optional mint and serve.

## Grapefruit and Orange Compote

In this compote, a mixture of honey and orange liqueur glosses sections of winter citrus. And dried dates, cut into nuggets, add a mellow sweetness to the orange and grapefruit. Fresh dates, if you can get them, are also delicious folded into the fruit.

[SERVES 4]

*¹/₄ cup honey, or to taste*
*3 tablespoons orange*
*  liqueur*
*4 pink grapefruit, peeled and*
*  cut into wedges*

*4 large seedless (navel)*
*  oranges, peeled and cut into*
*  segments*
*¹/₂ cup (about 3 ounces) pitted*
*  dates, cut into ¹/₃-inch pieces*

Combine the honey and orange liqueur in a bowl, stirring until the honey dissolves. Add the grapefruit wedges and orange segments, along with any juices that have accumulated as you cut the fruit. Scatter the dates over and toss carefully. Spoon helpings of the compote into individual bowls and serve. (The compote may be made up to 5 hours in advance and stored in the refrigerator.)

# Prune Compote

This fragrant compote is good to have on hand for serving with slices of lemon or spice pound cake.

[SERVES 6 TO 8]

*8 whole allspice berries*
*6 whole cloves*
*1/3 cup granulated sugar*
*1 1/4 cups red wine*
*1 cup water*

*1 small vanilla bean*
*3 cups (about 1 pound, 2 ounces) moist, plump prunes*
*Sour cream (optional)*

Tie up the allspice berries and cloves in a square of washed cheesecloth. Place the spice bundle, sugar, red wine, water, and vanilla bean in a medium-sized nonreactive casserole. Cover, place over low heat, and cook until the sugar dissolves completely; uncover, raise the heat to high, and boil for 1 minute.

Add the prunes to the syrup, cover, and simmer for about 20 minutes, or until tender; baste the prunes with the syrup from time to time.

Transfer the casserole to a cooling rack, uncover, and cool completely. Remove and discard the spice bundle, leaving in the vanilla bean for extra flavor. The prunes can be used now, or transfer them to a storage container, cover, and refrigerate for up to 1 month.

Serve the prunes warm, at room temperature, or chilled in compote glasses or bowls with some of the poaching liquid spooned over. Top each serving with a dollop of sour cream, if you like.

# Orange-Stewed Quince

To give this compote a sweet-sharp flavor, use a good orange marmalade that includes threads of the rind.

[SERVES 4]

4 quince, peeled, halved,
    cored, and cut into 2-inch
    chunks
1/3 cup orange marmalade
1/3 cup granulated sugar

1 teaspoon finely grated
    orange peel
1 1/2 cups freshly squeezed
    orange juice

Combine the chunks of quince, marmalade, sugar, and orange peel in a medium-sized nonreactive casserole (preferably enameled cast iron). Pour over the orange juice and toss. Cover the casserole and bring the contents to a simmer. Simmer the fruit for 30 to 40 minutes, or until tender.

Transfer the casserole to a cooling rack. Serve the compote warm, at room temperature, or chilled. (The compote may be stored in the refrigerator for up to 1 week.)

# Mélange of Dried Fruit
## with Cinnamon Crème Fraîche

The mélange stores well in the refrigerator for at least three weeks, where it will continue to mellow. Enjoy the fruit with wedges of vanilla pound cake, spice cake, or any other good butter cake.

[SERVES 8]

1½ cups dry red wine
1⅓ cups water
⅓ cup granulated sugar
8 strips fresh lemon peel
8 strips fresh orange peel
2 cinnamon sticks
1 small vanilla bean
4 whole allspice berries
4 whole cloves
1 cup (about 8 ounces) dried whole figs

1½ cups (about 6 ounces) dried peach halves
1 cup (about 4 ounces) dried pear halves
1 cup (about 6 ounces) dried apricot halves
½ cup (about 3 ounces) pitted dates
⅓ cup (about 2 ounces) golden raisins

**For the cinnamon crème fraîche:**

½ cup crème fraîche
3 tablespoons pure maple syrup blended with ¼ teaspoon ground cinnamon

½ teaspoon pure vanilla extract

Place the red wine, water, sugar, lemon peel, orange peel, cinnamon sticks, vanilla bean, allspice berries, and cloves in a large nonreactive casserole. Cover, place over low heat, and cook until the sugar has dissolved completely. Uncover, raise the heat to high, and bring the contents of the casserole to a boil. Boil for 1 minute.

*Fruit Desserts*

Add the figs, cover, and simmer for 10 minutes. Add the peaches, pears, and apricots; simmer for an additional 20 minutes, or until the fruit is tender. Remove the fruit to a bowl with a slotted spoon, discarding any citrus peel or spices that may be clinging to the fruit.

Boil the syrup for 1 minute, then strain out all of the spices except the cinnamon sticks and vanilla bean. Pour the syrup over the fruit, nestling the cinnamon sticks and vanilla bean among the pieces of fruit. Stir in the dates and raisins. Use the fruit warm, at room temperature, or chilled.

For the cinnamon crème fraîche, blend the crème fraîche, maple syrup–cinnamon mixture, and vanilla in a bowl. Stir well.

Spoon helpings of the fruit mélange into individual serving bowls and top each with a dollop of the crème fraîche sauce.

*Compotes and Salads*

# Rhubarb Compote

This compote is delightful served warm, with a pitcher of heavy cream for pouring over each serving.

[SERVES 6]

½ cup superfine sugar, or
more to taste
½ cup freshly squeezed orange
juice
6 strips orange peel
1 cinnamon stick

2 pounds trimmed rhubarb,
each stalk halved
lengthwise and cut into
1½-inch sections (about 4
cups)
About 1 cup heavy cream

Combine the sugar, orange juice, orange peel, cinnamon stick, and rhubarb in a medium-sized nonreactive casserole (preferably enameled cast iron). Cover, bring to a rapid simmer, and cook over low heat for about 15 minutes, or until the rhubarb is tender, stirring once or twice.

When the rhubarb is tender, remove the casserole from the heat, discard the cinnamon stick, pick out the strips of orange peel, and sweeten the rhubarb further, if you like, with extra superfine sugar. Cool the compote slightly and serve warm, or cool completely and serve at room temperature. (The rhubarb may be made up to 1 week in advance and refrigerated in a covered container.)

Serve helpings of the compote with heavy cream.

NOTE: Stalks of rhubarb generally come to market stripped of leaves; the leaves are poisonous and should not be eaten or used in cooking.

### Variation

For *Strawberry-Rhubarb Compote,* add 1 cup hulled and thickly sliced strawberries to the rhubarb compote after it has cooled completely. Serve immediately.

# Strawberries in Red Wine Syrup

This is a fine dessert to serve at an al fresco dinner. Accompany the berries with a bowl of crème fraîche and pass a plate of nut or spice cookies with the berries, if you like.

[SERVES 6]

**For the red wine syrup:**

*1 cup red wine*
*1 cup water*
*½ cup granulated sugar*
*2 cinnamon sticks*

*12 whole black peppercorns*
*6 whole allspice berries*
*6 whole cloves*

*3 pints red, ripe strawberries, hulled*

*Fresh mint sprigs (optional)*

For the red wine syrup, place the red wine, water, sugar, cinnamon sticks, peppercorns, allspice berries, and cloves in a medium-sized nonreactive saucepan. Cover, set over low heat, and cook until the sugar has dissolved completely. Uncover, bring to a boil, and boil for 5 to 7 minutes, or until slightly reduced.

Remove from the heat and cool completely. Remove and discard the peppercorns, allspice berries, and one of the cinnamon sticks. (The syrup may be prepared 5 days in advance; refrigerate in a tightly covered container.)

Place the strawberries in a serving bowl, pour over the syrup, and toss gently. Let the berries marinate in the syrup for at least 30 minutes before serving. (The cinnamon stick may be left in with the berries, for extra flavor.)

Ring the strawberries with the fresh mint sprigs, if you like, and serve.

# Figs in Bourbon-Vanilla Syrup

This syrup is useful to have on hand to glamorize such fruit as figs or ripe peach or nectarine halves. For serving, I like to encircle the edge of the plate with wisps of fresh mint and offer dollops of whipped cream (or crème fraîche) with each helping.

[SERVES 6]

**For the bourbon-vanilla syrup:**

*1 cup water*
*¼ cup good bourbon*
*¼ cup granulated sugar*
*6 whole allspice berries*

*1 small vanilla bean, slit down the middle to expose the tiny seeds*

*12 fresh figs, stemmed and halved*

*Whipped cream or crème fraîche (optional)*

For the bourbon-vanilla syrup, place the water, bourbon, sugar, allspice berries, and vanilla bean in a large nonreactive saucepan. Cover, place over low heat, and cook until the sugar dissolves completely. Uncover, raise the heat to high, and bring to the boil; boil for 2 minutes. Remove the saucepan from the heat.

Add the fig halves and spoon the syrup over and about them. (The vanilla bean and allspice berries can be removed, or left in to flavor the syrup further.) Continue to spoon the syrup over and about the figs a few more times.

Let the figs stand at room temperature for at least 1 hour. Just before serving, discard the allspice berries. Arrange 4 fig halves on each dessert plate, douse with a little of the syrup, and garnish with a dollop of whipped cream or crème fraîche, if you like.

*Fruit Desserts*

*Variation*

For *Dried Figs in Bourbon-Vanilla Syrup*, make the syrup with only 1 tablespoon granulated sugar. Simmer 1½ cups (about 12 ounces) dried figs in the syrup, covered, for 20 minutes, or until the figs are tender. Cool the figs in the syrup, then remove and discard the spices.

## Figs in Orange Juice

This simple treatment of figs—bathed in orange juice and a dash of honey—brings out the clear, fresh taste of the fruit.

[SERVES 4]

*12 fresh figs, stemmed and
  halved*
*1 cup freshly squeezed orange
  juice*

*1 tablespoon honey, or to
  taste*

Place the figs in a bowl. Pour over the orange juice. Drizzle over the honey. Carefully toss the figs in the liquid. Let stand at room temperature for 15 minutes, or up to 1 hour, to allow the flavors to merge.

Serve the figs in bowls and spoon some of the orange juice over each helping.

# Strawberries Cardinal

If fresh raspberries are unavailable, use frozen raspberries processed without sugar or sugar syrup.

[SERVES 5]

For the raspberry sauce:

*1¼ cups red, ripe raspberries, picked over*
*2 teaspoons freshly squeezed lemon juice*

*2 tablespoons raspberry jelly*
*3 tablespoons water*
*2 teaspoons cherry brandy*

*3 cups strawberries, hulled*

For the whipped cream topping:

*¾ cup cold heavy cream*

*2 teaspoons unsifted confectioners' sugar*

*2 tablespoons lightly toasted sliced or slivered almonds (optional)*

For the raspberry sauce, combine the raspberries, lemon juice, jelly, water, and brandy in a small nonreactive saucepan. Cover, place over moderate heat, and cook, stirring occasionally, for 15 to 20 minutes, or until the raspberries have broken down completely. Uncover the saucepan and cook for 2 minutes longer.

Purée the contents of the saucepan through a food mill fitted with the fine disk. Cool the raspberry sauce, transfer to a storage container, cover, and refrigerate. (The raspberry sauce may be made at least 1 week in advance.)

Toss the strawberries with the raspberry sauce.

For the whipped cream topping, beat the cream until it just begins to mound, add the confectioners' sugar, and continue beating until soft peaks form.

For each serving, pile a helping of berries in a compote dish or small bowl. Top the berries with a spoonful of the whipped cream and, if you are using them, scatter some of the toasted almonds on top. Serve immediately.

## Peaches in Sparkling White Wine

The ideal time to make this compote is during August, when juicy freestone peaches appear at the farm stands.

[SERVES 6]

6 ripe peaches, peeled, halved, pitted, and sliced
2 tablespoons honey, or to taste

2 cups chilled sparkling white wine

Place the peach slices and honey in a serving bowl. Toss gently. Pour over the sparkling wine and toss again. Let stand for 15 minutes. Spoon the peaches into serving bowls or compote dishes, along with some of the wine. Serve immediately.

NOTE: Either white or yellow peaches may be used.

# Applesauce

Applesauce is a compote of lightly sweetened apples cooked until very tender and thickened. A fine applesauce can be made in no time, and it can also serve as a luxurious base for the addition of poached fresh fruit, such as apricots, pears, or peaches, or dried fruit (prunes, apricots, figs, or raisins).

Plain applesauce is delicious served warm, with soft oatmeal cookies.

**[SERVES 6]**
*Makes about 3¾ cups, 4½ cups with the dried fruit added*

8 firm, crisp cooking apples (about 3 pounds), peeled, cored, and cut into chunks
¼ cup water, or more if needed
⅓ cup superfine sugar, or to taste
½ cup apple cider, or apple juice
1 tablespoon freshly squeezed lemon juice
1 cinnamon stick
½ teaspoon freshly grated nutmeg

Place the apple chunks, water, sugar, apple cider, lemon juice, and cinnamon stick in a large nonreactive saucepan or casserole (preferably enameled cast iron). Cover and cook over moderate heat, stirring now and again, until the mixture begins to bubble. Reduce the heat to low and continue cooking until the apples are very tender when pierced with the tip of a knife, about 20 minutes. If the apples are a little dry, you will have to add a few tablespoons more water as the sauce cooks.

Remove the pan from the heat, uncover, and lightly crush the apples with the back of a spoon or a potato masher. Stir in the nutmeg. Taste the sauce and adjust the sweetness, adding more sugar to taste, a teaspoon at at time.

Serve the applesauce warm or at room temperature.

## Variation

*Susan Friedland's Applesauce:* This recipe for applesauce comes from my editor. Nothing interferes with its clear, pure apple taste. She notes that ". . . with the wonderful assortment of apples available in the fall, it can be a fat- and sugar-free dessert." (A variation of this recipe appears in *The Jewish-American Kitchen* by Raymond Sokolov, recipes by Susan R. Friedland [New York: Stewart, Tabori and Chang, 1989]. And, in the same volume, don't miss her apple coffeecake—a delicious mingling of butter-rich yeast dough, chopped apples, cinnamon, raisins, and walnuts.)

Wash the cooking apples and cut the unpeeled fruit into rough chunks. Place the chunks in a casserole, cover, and cook over moderate heat until tender, about 30 minutes. (Occasionally, Susan adds a few strips of lemon peel to flavor the apples as they cook.) Purée the apples, with all the cooking juices, in a food mill fitted with the medium disk, leaving the peels and seeds behind. Flavor the applesauce with a pinch of cinnamon or nutmeg, and a little sugar to taste, if needed. Based on the types of apples you use, the skins will tint the sauce. Lovely.

## Fresh and Dried Fruit Additions

Here is a sampler of ingredients for enriching several cupfuls of applesauce. Besides the fruits discussed below, think of mixing fresh pineapple chunks, apricots, dried cherries (or mirabelles), or chopped, poached apricots into a batch of applesauce.

If you are making a basic applesauce in advance, and wish to add dried fruit later on, refer to the instructions below for plumping (or lightly simmering) the fruit separately. Otherwise, you can add the raisins, dates, diced prunes, figs, or diced dried apricots (or dried pears and peaches) directly to the sauce while it is still

*(continued)*

very hot. The fruit will plump up nicely as the applesauce cools down.

For the pear variation, you will need to poach chunks of the fruit in liquid before adding to the finished applesauce. The easiest way to do so is to make a syrup out of a fruit juice and lemon peel, and use this for the poaching liquid. For the *Fruit Juice Syrup*, combine 2 cups apple juice and 5 strips lemon peel in a medium-sized nonreactive saucepan. Bring the liquid to a simmer and add the prepared fruit.

For *Prune-Applesauce*, cover ⅔ cup (about 4 ounces) prunes with hot tea. Let stand for 15 minutes. Pat dry, pit, and cut into small pieces. Fold through the applesauce.

For *Dried Apricot–Applesauce*, plump ½ cup (3 ounces) dried apricot halves in 1 cup hot apple juice for 10 minutes. Drain the apricots, cut into quarters, and fold through the applesauce.

For *Pear-Applesauce*, peel, halve, and core 2 firm but ripe pears (such as Bosc or d'Anjou). Poach the pear halves in simmering Fruit Juice Syrup for about 7 to 10 minutes, or until just tender. Drain the pears, cut into small chunks, and fold through the applesauce.

For *Fig-Applesauce*, stem ½ cup (about 4 ounces) dried figs and simmer them in 1½ cups apple juice for 10 to 12 minutes, or until tender. Drain the figs, cut into small pieces, and fold through the applesauce.

For *Raisin and Date Applesauce*, plump ⅓ cup (about 2 ounces) golden raisins in ½ cup hot apple juice for 3 or 4 minutes. Drain well. Fold the raisins and ⅓ cup (about 2¼ ounces) diced pitted dates through the applesauce.

# Summer Berry Bowl

This no-cook dessert is quickly assembled—a real boon for the summertime cook who's in a hurry. To gussy up the presentation, tie a bundle of fresh mint (apple mint, spearmint, or peppermint) with a length of raffia and place it atop the berries.

[SERVES 6]

1/4 cup honey, or to taste (according to the sweetness of the berries)
1 cup white grape juice
1/2 cup apricot nectar, or apple juice
2 cups cherries, stemmed and pitted
2 cups blueberries, picked over

1 1/2 cups red or golden raspberries, picked over
1 1/2 cups black raspberries, picked over
1 cup blackberries, picked over
1 cup small strawberries, hulled

Whisk the honey, grape juice, and apricot nectar in a small mixing bowl. Place the cherries, blueberries, red raspberries, black raspberries, blackberries, and strawberries in a large serving bowl. Pour over the honey-nectar mixture and toss carefully.

Spoon the fruits into bowls and serve.

# 2

# Pies and Cakes, Tarts, Turnovers, and Dumplings

*Flaky Pie Crust*

*Apple Pie with Walnuts and Spices*

*Deep-Dish Summer Fruit Pie*

*Shredded Chocolate and Banana Cake*

*Pear Loaf Cake*

*Apple Snacking Cake*

*Orange-Rum Butter Cake with Glazed Orange Slices*

*Pear-Almond Tart*

*Prune Tart*
*Variations: Apple Tart, Blackberry Tart, Italian Prune Plum Tart*

*Lemon Cream Meringue Tart*

*Apple Meringue Tart*
*Variations: Peach Meringue Tart, Pear Meringue Tart,*
*Cherry Meringue Tart, Blueberry Meringue Tart*

Fresh Fruit Tart

Mango Cream Tart

Giant Peach Empanadas

Pear Foldover

Apple Dumplings
Variation: Pear Dumplings

With all the usual dairy staples and dry goods stocked in the pantry and refrigerator, and a pile of fresh fruit sitting on the kitchen counter, you can bake up a whole range of desserts that taste vibrant and fresh. There's nothing quite like the aroma of a fruit pie when it's just pulled from the oven, or the taste of a buttery slice of cake dotted with fresh fruit.

The pies, tarts, and dumplings in this chapter are all made from a batch or two of Flaky Pie Crust. The dough is very easy to manage and can be rolled out into rounds, wrapped tightly, and stashed in the freezer, all ready for those times when you come home with a heap of fruit and want to make a pie in a hurry.

Slices of cake or pie look pretty sitting on good china decorated with tiny flowers or fruit, on plain white dishes, or on pastel-colored glass plates. A footed cake stand can be used to show off your good-looking sweet. And an antique pie tin is ideal to use when baking and serving a pie.

# The Fruit Pies of Summer

Most any kind of fruit can be made into a luscious pie filling, keeping this general formula in mind: For a 9- or 10-inch double-crust pie, prepare two recipes of Flaky Pie Crust (you will have a little more pastry dough than you need, but this makes working with the dough easier). Roll out the dough between sheets of wax paper according to the directions on page 32. For each 3¾ to 4 cups of fruit (such as sliced fruit, a mixture of fruit and berries, or berries alone), combine 1 cup granulated sugar with 1 tablespoon of cornstarch (add an extra teaspoon if the fruit is especially juicy) and ½ teaspoon of ground spice, such as nutmeg (for apricots), cinnamon (for blueberries or blackberries), or ginger (for pears, peaches, nectarines, and plums). Toss the fruit with the sugar-flour-spice blend and 1 tablespoon freshly squeezed lemon juice. Let the filling stand for 10 minutes.

Line the bottom of the pie pan with one sheet of pastry dough according to the directions on page 33. Spoon in the fruit filling and dot the top with 1 tablespoon cold unsalted butter, cut into small bits. Using the second round of dough, prepare a cover of pastry dough cutouts according to the directions on page 34, and top the fruit with those cutouts. Chill the pie for 10 minutes. Brush the cutouts with ice-cold water and sprinkle over a little granulated sugar.

Bake the pie on a rack in the lower third of a preheated 425-degree oven for 20 minutes. Reduce the oven temperature to 375 degrees and continue baking for about 25 minutes longer, or until the crust is golden and the fruit is tender. Remove the pie to a cooling rack. Serve warm or at room temperature.

# Flaky Pie Crust

For pie- and tart-making, you'll need a reliable pastry dough—one that's light and flaky, firm yet meltingly tender, and a breeze to prepare. Over the years I perfected just the right formula for a pie crust that meets those standards and published it in *Country Pies: A Seasonal Sampler* (Harper & Row Publishers, Inc., 1988), the first of three books on the subject of country baking.

Flaky Pie Crust is quite adaptable. It can be used for pie and tart shells, and even for turnovers. The dough can be doubled successfully and used for double-crusted pies. It is made entirely with butter, but solid shortening can replace all or part of the butter, if you wish.

This recipe makes one 9- or 10-inch single-crust pie shell, or one 9- or 10-inch tart shell.

*1½ cups unsifted all-purpose flour (measured by stirring the flour gently to aerate it, scooping down into the flour with a dry measure, then leveling the top with the straight edge of a knife)*
*¼ teaspoon salt*

*8 tablespoons (1 stick) cold unsalted butter, cut into chunks (or substitute margarine)*
*1 tablespoon granulated sugar*
*1 cold extra-large egg yolk*
*2 tablespoons ice water, or more as needed*

*To make the dough by hand,* stir the flour and salt together in a large mixing bowl. Add the butter and, using 2 round-bladed knives, cut the fat into the flour until it is reduced to small pieces. Further blend the fat into the flour using your fingertips: Dip down into the mixture and crumble as you are lifting it to the surface. The mixture should look like coarse cornmeal. Sprinkle over the sugar and stir it in with a few brief strokes. Blend the egg yolk and water in a small bowl. Pour over the flour mixture. Quickly com-

bine everything to make a firm but pliable dough, using your fingertips or a fork. Add droplets of ice-cold water if the dough seems too dry or crumbly. Turn out the dough onto a large sheet of wax paper, shape into a rough, flat cake and wrap with the paper. Refrigerate for 15 to 20 minutes so the dough has an opportunity to relax.

A double recipe of this pie crust can be made by hand in one batch. Divide the dough into two cakes for chilling.

*To make the dough in a food processor,* place the flour and salt in the work bowl of a food processor fitted with the steel blade. Add the chunks of butter and process, using quick on-off pulses, until the butter is reduced to small flakes. Sprinkle with the sugar and process for 1 or 2 seconds to blend. Beat the egg yolk and water in a small mixing bowl and pour over the flour-butter mixture. Process, using short on-off pulses, until the dough *just* begins to mass together. Add extra drops of water if the dough seems crumbly or dry. Turn out the dough onto a large sheet of wax paper, shape into a flat cake, and wrap with the paper. Refrigerate for 15 to 20 minutes so the dough has an opportunity to relax.

When using a food processor for making pie crust, I prefer to make one batch of dough at a time.

*To roll out the pie or tart dough,* tear off two sheets of wax paper about 17 or 18 inches long. Place the dough in the center of one sheet of paper and top with the remaining sheet. Gently press down on the top sheet. With a rolling pin, roll out the dough to a scant ⅛-inch thickness (approximately 12 or 13 inches in diameter) using short, quick motions. Transfer the dough, between the sheets of wax paper, to a cookie sheet, and chill for 30 minutes. If you are doubling the recipe in order to make a top crust or two large turnovers (as in the recipe for Giant Peach Empanadas on page 60), divide the dough in half and roll out each half separately.

*To line a rimmed pie pan with a sheet of dough,* peel off the top layer of wax paper from the sheet of pie crust. Cut enough 1/3-inch-wide strips of dough from the outer edge of the dough to encircle the entire rim. Lightly brush the rim of the pan with ice water, press the strips onto the rim, and brush with ice water. Invert the circle of dough onto the bottom of the pan and carefully peel off the wax paper. Press the dough lightly into the bottom first, then up and against the sides. Press the overhang of dough onto the rim and cut off the overhang, using a sharp paring knife. Make long 1/16-inch-deep scoring marks on the outside edges of the dough to give texture to the rim and give it a bit of thickness. Crimp the edges with the tines of a fork.

Prick the bottom of the pie shell with the tines of a fork. Refrigerate for 30 minutes. For longer storage, enclose the pan in a sheet of plastic wrap, slide into a large plastic bag, seal, and refrigerate. Save the scraps of dough in a separate bag to use for patching, if necessary. The pastry-lined pie pan can be stored safely in the refrigerator for up to 3 days.

*To line a tart pan with a sheet of dough,* peel off the wax paper from the sheet of dough. Invert the circle of dough onto a tart pan. (I use tart pans with removable or false bottoms; they have fluted sides and are made out of tinned steel.) Press the dough lightly on the bottom first, then up and against the sides. Using the overhang of dough and your thumb, press 1/4-inch sections of dough back into the edges of the pan. Roll a rolling pin over the surface of the tart pan to cut away the overhang of dough. Peel away the overhang and reserve the extra dough in case you need it to patch the crust. Press up the sides with your thumb and forefinger to extend the dough a scant 1/4 inch higher than the rim of the tart pan.

Prick the bottom of the tart shell with the tines of a fork. Refrigerate for 30 minutes. For longer storage, enclose the pan in a

*Pies and Cakes, Tarts, Turnovers, and Dumplings*

sheet of plastic wrap, slide into a large plastic bag, seal, and refrigerate. Keep the scraps of dough in a separate bag. The pastry-lined tart pan can be stored safely in the refrigerator for up to 3 days.

*To freeze an unbaked sheet of pastry dough,* wrap in several sheets of plastic wrap, slide into a large self-sealing plastic bag, and freeze. The sheet of dough should be used within 2 or 3 months. Transfer it from the freezer to the refrigerator and use when pliable, about 6 to 8 hours.

*To freeze an unbaked pie or tart shell,* wrap in several sheets of plastic wrap, slide into a self-sealing plastic bag, and freeze. The pie or tart shell should be used within 2 or 3 months; bake directly from the freezer without defrosting.

For a frozen single-crust pie or tart shell, increase the baking time at 375 degrees by 5 or 6 minutes, or until the shell is a golden brown color.

*To fashion a pie cover of pastry cutouts,* select a cookie cutter for stamping out the cutouts: Diamonds, hearts, scalloped rounds, triangles, rectangles, animals, or fruits are all distinctive shapes. Stamp cutouts from the second sheet of pie dough and chill them on a cookie sheet. After the filling has been piled into the pie shell, cover the top with the cutouts, overlapping one on the next to form a top crust. Since some small patches of filling will show through, cutting steam vents in the top crust is unnecessary. Chill the pie for 10 minutes and bake as directed.

*To cover a deep-dish pie with a round of pie dough,* peel off the top layer of wax paper from the sheet of pie crust. Cut ⅓-inch-wide strips of dough from the outer edge of the circle of dough. Lightly brush the rim of a 9-inch ovenproof oval or round deep-dish pie pan with cold water. Press on the strips of dough. Spoon the filling

into the pie dish, mounding it slightly. Brush the top of the pastry-lined rim with ice water. Lay the pie crust over the filling by inverting the circle of dough over the filled pie pan. Carefully peel away the sheet of wax paper. Press the dough firmly on the rim. Cut away any overhang of dough with a sharp paring knife. Make long, $^1/_{16}$-inch scoring marks on the outside edges of the dough to give texture to the rim and give it some thickness. Flute or crimp the edges decoratively. Refrigerate the pie for 10 minutes, then bake.

*To completely prebake a pie or tart shell,* line the well-chilled pie or tart shell with a single length of aluminum foil. Fill with raw rice or dried beans. Preheat the oven to 425 degrees. Place a cookie sheet on a rack set in the lower third of the oven, and place the pie shell on the cookie sheet. Bake the pie or tart shell for 10 minutes, carefully remove the foil with the rice and beans, reduce the oven temperature to 375 degrees, and continue baking for 10 to 12 minutes longer, or until baked through and golden (medium amber) color.

*Pies and Cakes, Tarts, Turnovers, and Dumplings*

# Apple Pie with Walnuts and Spices

Lightly toasted chopped walnuts tossed with sweetened and spiced apple slices make up the simple filling for this pie. Serve slices of pie with scoops of vanilla ice cream or drifts of whipped cream sweetened with a little confectioners' sugar.

[SERVES 6]

For the pastry dough:

*2 sheets pie dough made from*
*2 recipes Flaky Pie Crust*
*(see pages 31–35)*

For the filling:

*1 tablespoon plus 1 teaspoon*
*cornstarch*
*¾ cup granulated sugar*
*1 teaspoon ground cinnamon*
*¼ teaspoon ground allspice*
*¼ teaspoon freshly grated*
*nutmeg*
*Pinch salt*
*4¾ cups (about 3 pounds)*
*peeled, cored, and sliced*
*tart cooking apples*

*2 tablespoons freshly squeezed*
*lemon juice*
*1 teaspoon finely grated lemon*
*peel*
*½ cup lightly toasted chopped*
*walnuts*
*2 tablespoons unsalted butter,*
*cut into bits (or substitute*
*margarine)*

For the glaze:

*2 tablespoons cold water*

*2 teaspoons granulated sugar*

Have ready in the refrigerator a 10-inch pie pan lined with one sheet of the pie dough. Remove the second sheet of pie dough from the refrigerator so that it softens enough to cover the mound of apples.

Thoroughly combine the cornstarch, sugar, cinnamon, allspice, nutmeg, and salt in a large mixing bowl. Add the apple slices, lemon juice, lemon peel, and walnuts. Toss well. Pile the filling into the pie shell, mounding it slightly in the center. Dot the top of the filling with the bits of butter.

Peel off the top layer of wax paper from the second sheet of pie dough, invert the dough over the filling, and carefully peel away the wax paper. Press the two edges together to seal, then crimp the rim of dough decoratively. Cut a few steam vents in the top of the pastry cover with the tip of a sharp knife. Refrigerate the pie for 10 minutes.

Preheat the oven to 425 degrees.

For the glaze, brush the cold water lightly over the top of the pie and sprinkle over the granulated sugar.

Bake the pie on a rack set in the lower third of the preheated oven for 10 minutes. Reduce the oven temperature to 350 degrees and continue baking for about 40 minutes longer, or until the pastry is golden brown.

Transfer the pie to a cooling rack. Serve warm or at room temperature.

# Deep-Dish Summer Fruit Pie

This deep-dish pie holds plenty of sweetened summer fruit—sliced peaches, plums, apricots, and blueberries bake up tender and succulent under the buttery top crust. This pie is a good way to use up small amounts of perfectly ripe fruit that you may have on hand. It is delicious served as is, or with cold, creamy scoops of vanilla ice cream.

[SERVES 6]

For the fruit:

1 tablespoon all-purpose flour
¾ cup granulated sugar
1 tablespoon freshly squeezed
   lemon juice
1 cup blueberries, picked over
2 cups peeled, pitted, and
   sliced ripe peaches

1 cup pitted and quartered
   ripe apricots
1 cup pitted and sliced ripe
   red plums
1 tablespoon cold unsalted
   butter, cut into bits (or
   substitute margarine)

For the pastry dough:

1 sheet pie dough made from
   1 recipe Flaky Pie Crust
   (see pages 31–35)

For the glaze:

2 tablespoons ice water

2 teaspoons granulated sugar

Preheat the oven to 425 degrees.

For the fruit, thoroughly combine the flour and sugar in a large mixing bowl. Stir in the lemon juice, blueberries, peaches, apricots, and plums. Turn the fruit mixture into a 10-inch pie pan that is 3 inches deep. Dot the top with the bits of butter.

*Fruit Desserts*

For the pastry dough, cover the top of the fruit with the round of dough according to the directions on page 34. Refrigerate the pie for 10 minutes.

For the glaze, brush the top of the pie with the ice water and sprinkle with the sugar. Cut a few steam vents in the top crust with a small sharp knife.

Bake the pie on a rack in the lower third of the preheated oven for 15 minutes, reduce the oven temperature to 350 degrees, and continue baking for 35 minutes longer, or until the topping is a rich golden brown.

Transfer the pie to a cooling rack. Serve warm or at room temperature.

*Pies and Cakes, Tarts, Turnovers, and Dumplings*

# Shredded Chocolate and Banana Cake

Once you see how wonderfully moist mashed ripe bananas make a cake, you may be tempted to add them to other batters— for pancakes, waffles, muffins, cupcakes, and such. This is a light, full-flavored banana cake conveniently baked in a loaf pan; the batter is spotted with dark "crumbs" of bittersweet chocolate, which adds an intriguing taste to the finished sweet.

[SERVES 6]

1½ cups unsifted all-purpose flour
½ cup unsifted cake flour
1 teaspoon baking soda
¼ teaspoon baking powder
¼ teaspoon salt
¾ cup grated bittersweet chocolate (use a good bar chocolate such as Lindt Excellence or Tobler Tradition) (see Baking Note)
3 medium-sized fully ripe bananas, at room temperature
¼ cup buttermilk, at room temperature

2 teaspoons pure vanilla extract
6 tablespoons unsalted butter, softened at room temperature (or substitute margarine)
2 tablespoons shortening
1 cup Vanilla-Scented Granulated Sugar (page 173)
2 extra-large eggs, at room temperature
Confectioners' sugar (optional)

Lightly butter and flour a 9 x 5 x 3-inch loaf pan. Set aside. Preheat the oven to 325 degrees.

Sift the all-purpose flour, cake flour, baking soda, baking powder, and salt onto a sheet of wax paper. Place the grated chocolate in a bowl and stir in 1 teaspoon of the sifted mixture; set aside. Mash the bananas in a bowl (there should be about 1 generous cup), then stir in the buttermilk and vanilla; set aside.

*Fruit Desserts*

Cream the butter and shortening in the large bowl of an electric mixer on moderate speed for 3 or 4 minutes. Raise the speed to moderately high, add half of the sugar, and beat for 1 minute; add the remaining sugar and beat for 1 minute longer, scraping down the sides and bottom of the bowl to keep the mixture even-textured. Add the eggs, one at a time, beating well after each addition. Blend in the banana-buttermilk mixture on low speed (the buttermilk will cause the mixture to appear slightly curdled, but this is to be expected). On low speed, blend in the flour mixture in 2 additions, beating just until the particles of flour have been absorbed. By hand, stir in the chocolate.

Pour and scrape the batter into the prepared pan. Bake the cake on a rack in the middle or lower third of the preheated oven for 55 minutes to 1 hour, or until risen, golden brown on top, and a wooden pick inserted in the center of the cake emerges clean and dry.

Transfer the pan to a cooling rack and let stand for 3 or 4 minutes. Carefully invert onto a second rack, remove the pan, and invert the cake again to cool right side up.

Sift confectioners' sugar generously over the top, if you like, and cut the cake into thick slices with a serrated knife. Serve the cake plain, with vanilla ice cream and hot fudge sauce, or with a fresh banana compote.

BAKING NOTE: To grate bittersweet bar chocolate, rub the bar over the large holes of a 4-sided box grater set over a bowl. Alternatively, finely chop the chocolate by hand, using a large chef's knife, or chop in the bowl of a food processor fitted with the steel blade.

# Pear Loaf Cake

This is a fine-grained cake scented with freshly grated nutmeg and grated lemon peel. Over the years, this cake has appeared on my tea table, but recently I decided to serve it for dessert, along with a compote of poached pear wedges. The White Wine–Poached Pears on page 126 make an excellent accompaniment.

[SERVES 6]

*1 cup unsifted all-purpose flour*
*1/2 cup plus 2 tablespoons unsifted cake flour*
*1 teaspoon baking powder*
*1/4 teaspoon salt*
*1/4 teaspoon freshly grated nutmeg*
*8 tablespoons (1 stick) unsalted butter, softened at room temperature (or substitute margarine)*
*1 cup Lemon-Scented Granulated Sugar (page 173), or plain granulated sugar*

*2 extra-large eggs, separated, at room temperature*
*1 teaspoon finely grated lemon peel*
*1/2 cup milk blended with 1 teaspoon pure lemon extract and 1 tablespoon light cream, at room temperature*
*3/4 cup lightly packed peeled, cored, and shredded ripe pears*
*Confectioners' sugar (optional)*

Lightly butter and flour a 9 x 5 x 3-inch loaf pan. Set aside. Preheat the oven to 350 degrees.

Sift the all-purpose flour, cake flour, baking powder, salt, and nutmeg onto a sheet of wax paper. Cream the butter in the large bowl of an electric mixer on moderately high speed for 3 or 4 minutes. Add the granulated sugar in 2 additions, beating for 1 minute after each portion of sugar is added. Beat in the egg yolks, one at a time, beating well after each addition. Scrape down the

sides of the mixing bowl frequently to keep the batter even-textured. Blend in the lemon peel.

On low speed, add the sifted dry ingredients in 2 additions, alternating with the milk mixture. Stir in the shredded pears.

Whip the egg whites until firm (not stiff) peaks form. Stir a spoonful of the whites into the batter, then fold in the remaining whites.

Spoon the batter into the prepared loaf pan. Bake the loaf on a rack set in the lower third of the preheated oven for 50 to 55 minutes, or until firm to the touch, golden, and a wooden pick inserted in the center emerges without any clinging cake particles. (The baked cake will pull away slightly from the edges of the loaf pan.)

Transfer the pan to a cooling rack and let stand for 3 or 4 minutes. Invert onto a second rack, lift off the pan, then invert the cake to cool right side up. Cool completely.

Sprinkle the top of the cake with confectioners' sugar, if you like. Cut the loaf into medium-thick slices with a serrated knife. Serve topped with lightly sweetened whipped cream or scatter a few poached pear wedges to the side of each piece of cake.

# Apple Snacking Cake

The texture of this apple cake is feathery and delicate, which makes it ideal for serving as a light dessert or in the afternoon with iced tea or hot cider, depending upon the weather. It also makes a superb breakfast cake, cut into thick fingers.

[SERVES 6]

**For the apples:**

1½ tablespoons unsalted butter (or substitute margarine)

2 firm, tart cooking apples, peeled, cored, and sliced

1 teaspoon freshly squeezed lemon juice

1 tablespoon granulated sugar blended with ¼ teaspoon ground cinnamon

1 tablespoon moist dried currants

**For the cake batter:**

1¼ cups unsifted all-purpose flour

¼ cup unsifted cake flour

1 teaspoon baking powder

¼ teaspoon baking soda

¼ teaspoon salt

½ teaspoon ground cinnamon

¼ teaspoon freshly grated nutmeg

6 tablespoons (¾ stick) unsalted butter, softened at room temperature (or substitute margarine)

2 tablespoons vegetable shortening

1 cup Vanilla-Scented Granulated Sugar (page 173), or plain granulated sugar

2 extra-large eggs, separated, at room temperature

1½ teaspoons pure vanilla extract

5 tablespoons light cream, at room temperature

Lightly butter an 8 x 8 x 2-inch cake pan. Line the bottom of the pan with a square of wax paper and dust the sides of the pan with a little flour. Set aside. Preheat the oven to 350 degrees.

For the apples, heat the butter in a skillet and add the apple slices and lemon juice; stir-cook over moderate heat 2 or 3 minutes. Sprinkle over the sugar-cinnamon blend and continue to cook until the apples are barely tender and glazed, about 1 or 2 minutes. Stir in the currants, cool slightly, and spoon into the bottom of the prepared cake pan. Set aside.

For the cake batter, sift the all-purpose flour, cake flour, baking powder, baking soda, salt, cinnamon, and nutmeg onto a sheet of wax paper.

Cream the butter and shortening in the large bowl of an electric mixer on moderately high speed for 2 or 3 minutes. Add ¾ cup granulated sugar, ¼ cup at a time, and beat for 1 minute after each addition. Beat in the egg yolks and vanilla. On low speed, add the sifted ingredients in 2 additions, alternating with the cream. Scrape down the sides of the mixing bowl frequently to keep the batter even-textured.

Beat the egg whites until soft peaks form. Add the remaining ¼ cup granulated sugar and continue beating until firm (not stiff) peaks form. Stir a large spoonful of the egg whites into the batter, then fold in the remaining whites. Pour and scrape the batter into the prepared baking pan, directly over the apples.

Bake the cake on a rack set in the lower third of the preheated oven for 45 to 50 minutes, or until golden and a wooden pick inserted into the center of the cake part emerges clean and dry.

Transfer the pan to a cooling rack and let stand for 1 minute. Run a thin, flexible palette knife around the edge of the cake, then invert onto a second cooling rack. Remove the cake pan and peel away the wax paper if it is clinging to the apples (sometimes it clings and sometimes it doesn't).

Serve the cake warm or at room temperature, cut into squares.

*Pies and Cakes, Tarts, Turnovers, and Dumplings*

# Orange-Rum Butter Cake
## with Glazed Orange Slices

The perfect time to make this cake is during the winter months, when thick-skinned navel oranges are available at the market.

[SERVES 12 TO 14]

**For the orange cake:**

2½ cups unsifted all-purpose
  flour
½ cup unsifted cake flour
1 tablespoon baking powder
½ teaspoon salt
¼ teaspoon ground allspice
¼ teaspoon ground cinnamon
½ pound (2 sticks) unsalted
  butter, softened at room
  temperature
2 cups Orange-Scented
  Granulated Sugar (page
  173)

2 tablespoons finely grated
  orange peel
4 extra-large eggs, at room
  temperature
2 extra-large egg yolks, at
  room temperature
½ cup freshly squeezed orange
  juice blended with ¼ cup
  dark rum and 1 teaspoon
  orange extract

**For the glazed orange slices:**

¼ cup dark rum
½ cup water
3 tablespoons granulated
  sugar

6 seedless (navel) oranges,
  peel and pith removed, cut
  into ⅓-inch-thick slices

Lightly butter and flour a 12-cup (10-inch) bundt pan. Set aside. Preheat the oven to 350 degrees.

For the bundt cake, sift the all-purpose flour, cake flour, baking powder, salt, allspice, and cinnamon onto a sheet of wax paper.

Cream the butter in the large bowl of an electric mixer on moderately high speed for 3 or 4 minutes. Add the scented sugar in 3 additions, beating for 1 minute after each portion is added. Beat in the orange peel. Beat in the eggs, one at a time, beating thoroughly after each addition. Beat in the egg yolks. Scrape down the sides of the mixing bowl frequently to keep the batter even-textured. On low speed, alternately add the sifted flour mixture in 3 additions with the orange juice–rum-extract in 2 additions, beginning with the sifted flour mixture.

Pour and scrape the batter into the prepared bundt pan. Shake the pan gently from side to side to level the batter. Bake the cake on a rack set in the lower third of the preheated oven for 50 minutes to 1 hour, or until golden brown, firm to the touch, and a wooden pick inserted into the cake emerges clean and dry. (The baked cake will pull away slightly from the sides of the baking pan.)

Transfer the pan to a cooling rack and let stand for 3 or 4 minutes. Invert onto a second cooling rack, lift off the pan, and let the cake cool completely.

For the glazed orange slices, place the rum, water, and sugar in a small saucepan. Cover, set over low heat, and cook until the sugar dissolves completely. Uncover, raise the heat to high, and bring to the boil. Boil 1 minute. Remove from the heat and set aside to cool completely.

Place the orange slices in a serving bowl and pour over the rum-charged syrup. Let stand for at least 15 minutes, spooning the syrup over the fruit now and again.

Cut the cake into slices, place each slice on a dessert plate, and overlap a few marinated orange slices to one side of each piece of cake. Serve immediately.

# Pear-Almond Tart

If you happen to have poached pears already on hand, by all means use them in place of the sautéed pears; thoroughly drain the cooked pears on paper towels and slice thickly.

[SERVES 6]

**For the pears:**

*1 tablespoon unsalted butter (or substitute margarine)*
*3 firm but ripe pears such as Bosc, peeled, cored, and thickly sliced*

*2 tablespoons maple syrup*
*¼ teaspoon freshly grated nutmeg*

**For the almond cream filling:**

*2 extra-large eggs, at room temperature*
*1 extra-large egg yolk, at room temperature*
*⅓ cup superfine sugar*
*⅔ cup sour cream, at room temperature*
*⅔ cup light cream, at room temperature*

*1 teaspoon pure vanilla extract*
*¼ teaspoon pure almond extract*
*¼ cup very finely chopped toasted almonds*

**For the pastry:**

*1 baked 9-inch tart shell, made from 1 recipe Flaky Pie Crust (see pages 31–35)*

Preheat the oven to 350 degrees.
For the pears, heat the butter in a skillet, add the sliced pears,

and cook over moderate heat for 2 or 3 minutes. Add the maple syrup and nutmeg, stir, and cook until the pears are just tender, about 1 or 2 minutes longer. Remove from the heat and set aside to cool.

For the almond cream filling, whisk together the eggs, egg yolk, and sugar in a large mixing bowl. Beat in the sour cream and light cream. Blend in the extracts and chopped almonds.

Spoon the cooled pears into the bottom of the baked tart shell, spreading them out in an even layer. Pour over the almond cream filling. Bake the tart on a rack in the lower third of the preheated oven for 25 minutes, or until the filling is slightly puffed and set.

Transfer the tart to a cooling rack.

Serve the tart warm or at room temperature, sliced into pie-shaped wedges.

# Prune Tart

This is a tart of contrasts: A creamy cheesecakelike filling is spooned into a tart shell strewn with plump prunes. The vanilla-flavored filling is a good contrast to the dried fruit.

[SERVES 6]

**For the prunes:**

*⅔ cup (about 4 ounces) prunes*     *1 cup strong hot tea*

**For the filling:**

*One 8-ounce package cream cheese, at room temperature*
*2 tablespoons unsalted butter, melted and cooled (or substitute margarine)*
*2 teaspoons unsifted cake flour*
*2 tablespoons ground almonds*
*½ cup Vanilla-Scented Superfine Sugar (page 173), or plain superfine sugar*

*2 extra-large eggs, at room temperature*
*1½ teaspoons pure vanilla extract*
*Pinch salt*
*½ cup sour cream, at room temperature*

**For the pastry:**

*1 baked 10-inch tart shell, made from 1 recipe Flaky Pie Crust (see pages 31–35)*

*Confectioners' sugar (optional)*

Preheat the oven to 350 degrees.
Place the prunes in a bowl and pour over the hot tea; let stand

for 30 minutes, or until the fruit is plump. Drain the prunes well and place them on several sheets of paper towels. Pat dry. Cut each prune into quarters and pit.

For the filling, beat the cream cheese and butter in the large bowl of an electric mixer on moderately high speed for 3 minutes; beat in the cake flour, almonds, and sugar. Beat in the eggs, one at a time; blend in the vanilla, salt, and sour cream. Scrape down the sides of the mixing bowl with a rubber spatula from time to time to keep the filling even-textured.

Arrange the prunes on the bottom of the baked tart shell. Spoon over the cream cheese filling, smoothing the top with a spatula or flexible palette knife. Bake the tart on a rack in the lower third of the preheated oven for 30 minutes, or until puffed and set (the topping will remain pale).

Transfer the tart to a cooling rack. Cool. The filling will lose some of its puffiness as it cools.

Let the tart stand for at least 1 hour before serving. If you wish, sift confectioners' sugar over the top of the tart before cutting into pie-shaped wedges.

## Variations

For *Apple Tart,* omit prunes and tea. Instead, sauté 2 tart cooking apples, peeled, cored, and diced, in 2 tablespoons butter for 3 minutes over moderate heat. Add ¼ cup apple cider or apple juice, 2 teaspoons sugar, 1 teaspoon cinnamon, and ¼ teaspoon freshly grated nutmeg; stir-cook for 2 minutes longer or until the apples are just tender. Raise the heat and cook for a few seconds to condense the cooking juices to a glaze. Transfer to a bowl and cool completely. Spoon the apple mixture into the baked tart shell, cover with the filling, and bake as directed.

(continued)

For *Blackberry Tart,* omit prunes and tea. Instead, strew ¾ cup firm, ripe blackberries over the bottom of the baked tart shell. Cover with the filling and bake as directed.

For *Italian Prune Plum Tart,* omit dried prunes and tea. Instead, halve, pit, and quarter 8 small ripe Italian prune plums. Sauté the plums in 1 tablespoon butter for 1 minute over moderate heat and arrange in the bottom of the baked tart shell. Cover with the filling and bake as directed.

## Lemon Cream Meringue Tart

This stovetop-cooked filling can also serve as a base for a top layer of fresh blueberries, small, whole strawberries, or raspberries.

[SERVES 6]

**For the lemon cream:**

2 tablespoons cornstarch
½ cup granulated sugar
Pinch salt
1 cup light cream
½ cup milk
¼ cup freshly squeezed lemon
  juice

3 extra-large egg yolks, at
  room temperature, beaten
1 teaspoon finely grated lemon
  peel
2 tablespoons cold unsalted
  butter (or substitute
  margarine)

**For the pastry dough:**

1 baked 9-inch tart shell, made
  from 1 recipe Flaky Pie
  Crust (see pages 31–35)

*Fruit Desserts*

**For the meringue topping:**

*3 extra-large egg whites (about ½ cup), at room temperature*

*Pinch cream of tartar*
*4½ tablespoons granulated sugar*

For the lemon cream filling, thoroughly combine the corn-starch, sugar, and salt in a medium-sized nonreactive saucepan (preferably enameled cast iron). Whisk in the light cream and milk. Bring the contents of the saucepan to a boil over moderately high heat, stirring slowly all the while. Reduce the heat and simmer for 3 minutes. Remove the saucepan from the heat and add the lemon juice. Blend a large spoonful of the hot cream mixture into the beaten egg yolks, then stir the egg yolk mixture into the cream mixture. Return the saucepan to the heat and simmer for 1 or 2 minutes, or until thickened. Blend in the lemon peel and butter.

Pour and scrape the lemon cream into the baked tart shell. Cool for 10 minutes.

Preheat the oven to 350 degrees.

For the meringue, place the egg whites and cream of tartar in a deep bowl and, using a hand-held electric mixer, beat until soft peaks form. Beat in the sugar, a little at a time, and continue beating until stiff peaks form. Spread the meringue over the lemon cream filling, making sure that the meringue touches the edges of the tart shell.

Bake the tart on a rack in the middle level of the preheated oven for 15 minutes, or until the meringue is firm, fully cooked, and golden.

Transfer the tart to a cooling rack. Cool completely. Serve the tart cut into pie-shaped wedges.

# Apple Meringue Tart

The filling for this tart consists of sliced apples baked in a vanilla-flavored custard. The tart is capped with a lightly sweetened meringue, an airy contrast to the apple custard.

[SERVES 6]

**For the filling:**

*¼ cup firmly packed light
brown sugar*
*1 tablespoon granulated sugar*
*1 extra-large egg, at room
temperature*
*1 extra-large egg yolk, at
room temperature*
*¼ teaspoon freshly grated
nutmeg*

*1 teaspoon pure vanilla
extract*
*¾ cup heavy cream, at room
temperature*
*2 large tart cooking apples,
peeled, cored, and thinly
sliced*

**For the pastry dough:**

*1 baked 9-inch tart shell, made
from 1 recipe Flaky Pie
Crust (see pages 31–35)*

**For the meringue topping:**

*3 extra-large egg whites (about
½ cup), at room
temperature*

*Pinch cream of tartar*
*4½ tablespoons granulated
sugar*

Preheat the oven to 350 degrees.

Whisk the light brown sugar, granulated sugar, egg, egg yolk, nutmeg, and vanilla extract in a mixing bowl. Beat in the heavy

cream. Arrange the apple slices on the bottom of the baked tart shell. Pour over the heavy cream mixture.

Bake the tart on a rack in the middle of the oven for about 40 minutes, or until the apples are tender and the custard is set.

Transfer the tart to a cooling rack. Let cool for 10 minutes.

Turn up the oven to 350 degrees.

For the meringue, place the egg whites and cream of tartar in a deep bowl and, using a hand-held electric mixer, beat to very soft peaks. Beat in the sugar, a little at a time, and continue beating until stiff peaks form. Spread the meringue over the baked tart, making sure that the meringue touches the edges of the tart shell.

Bake the tart on the middle rack of the preheated oven for 15 minutes, or until the meringue is firm, fully cooked, and golden.

Transfer the tart to a cooling rack. Cool completely. Serve the tart cut into pie-shaped wedges.

*Variations*

For *Peach Meringue Tart*, substitute for the apples 2 ripe peaches, peeled, halved, pitted, and sliced.

For *Pear Meringue Tart*, substitute for the apples 2 ripe pears, peeled, halved, pitted, and sliced.

For *Cherry Meringue Tart*, substitute for the apples 1¼ cups red cherries, stemmed, pitted, and halved.

For *Blueberry Meringue Tart*, substitute for the apples 1 cup blueberries, picked over.

# Fresh Fruit Tart

Consider this recipe a blueprint for the range of fruit tarts you can make using seasonal berries and whole, ripe fruit.

[SERVES 6 TO 8]

**For the vanilla cream filling:**

*2 tablespoons cornstarch*
*⅓ cup plus 1 tablespoon*
*granulated sugar*
*Pinch salt*
*1 cup milk, at room*
*temperature*
*⅔ cup heavy cream, at room*
*temperature*

*3 extra-large egg yolks, at*
*room temperature, beaten to*
*mix*
*2 tablespoons unsalted butter*
*(or substitute margarine)*
*1 teaspoon pure vanilla*
*extract*

**For the pastry dough:**

*1 baked 10-inch tart shell, made*
*from 1 recipe Flaky Pie*
*Crust (see pages 31–35)*

**For the glaze (choose one):**

## Apricot Glaze

(to use with peaches, nectarines, golden raspberries, and bananas, or on a mixed fruit tart)

*1¼ cups apricot preserves (use*
*the least expensive you can*
*find, with as few chunks of*
*fruit as possible, since the*
*preserves are strained of*
*any fruit pieces)*

*1 tablespoon water*
*2 teaspoons freshly squeezed*
*lemon juice*

*Fruit Desserts*

## Red Currant Jelly Glaze

(to use with strawberries, red and black raspberries, blackberries, plums, blueberries, and figs)

*1 cup red currant jelly*

**For the fruit:**

Choose from one or a combination of the following fruits, using about 3¾ cups fruit in total.

*Strawberries, hulled*
*Blackberries, picked over*
*Thickly sliced ripe bananas*
*Peeled, halved, pitted, and*
  *sliced ripe peaches, drained*
  *on paper towels*
*Halved, pitted, and sliced ripe*
  *nectarines, drained on*
  *paper towels*

*Halved, pitted, and thickly*
  *sliced ripe plums, drained*
  *on paper towels*
*Stemmed and thickly sliced*
  *ripe figs*
*Red raspberries, black*
  *raspberries, or golden*
  *raspberries, picked over*
*Blueberries, picked over*

For the vanilla cream filling, thoroughly combine the cornstarch, sugar, and salt in a medium-sized saucepan (preferably enameled cast iron). Whisk in the milk and heavy cream. Bring the contents of the saucepan to a boil over moderately high heat, whisking slowly all the while. Reduce the heat and simmer for 3 minutes. Remove the saucepan from the heat and blend a spoonful of the hot cream mixture into the egg yolks. Whisk the egg yolk mixture back into the cream mixture. Return the saucepan to the heat and simmer for 1 minute, or until thickened. Remove from the heat. Add the butter and vanilla, and stir until the butter melts completely. Strain through a fine-meshed sieve into a bowl.

Spoon the vanilla cream into the baked tart shell. Cool completely. *(continued)*

*Pies and Cakes, Tarts, Turnovers, and Dumplings*

To make the apricot glaze, place the preserves, water, and lemon juice in a small nonreactive saucepan, set over moderate heat, and bring to the boil. Reduce the heat and simmer for 2 minutes. Strain the mixture through a stainless-steel sieve. Use the glaze while it is still warm.

To make the red currant jelly glaze, place the jelly in a small nonreactive saucepan, set over moderately heat, and bring to the boil. Reduce the heat and simmer for 1 minute. Use the glaze while it is still hot.

To assemble the tart (up to 2 hours ahead), arrange the selected fruit attractively over the top of the filling (strawberries sitting hulled side down; sliced nectarines, plums, or peaches in concentric circles; sliced bananas or figs slightly overlapping). Crevices of the vanilla cream will peek through, which is fine.

Using a pastry brush, glaze the top of the tart: Scoop the bristles into the glaze and lavish on the glaze by dabbing it over and about the fruit. Actually brushing the glaze on the fruit will dislodge the fruit and never enrobe it in glaze.

Let the tart stand for 20 minutes to firm up the glaze (longer in a warm summer kitchen). Cut the tart into pie-shaped wedges.

## Mango Cream Tart

A large papaya, peeled, halved, seeded, and sliced, can be substituted for the mangoes.

[SERVES 6]

**3 tablespoons peach preserves,**
**warmed**

**For the pastry dough:**

*1 baked 9-inch tart shell, made
from 1 recipe Flaky Pie
Crust (see pages 31–35)*

**For the mango cream:**

*2 ripe mangoes, peeled and
sliced, slices drained on
paper towels
1 extra-large egg, at room
temperature
2 extra-large egg yolks, at
room temperature
1/4 cup firmly packed light
brown sugar*

*2 1/2 tablespoons granulated
sugar
1 teaspoon pure vanilla
extract
3/4 cup heavy cream, at room
temperature
1 tablespoon unsalted butter,
cut into bits (or substitute
margarine)*

Preheat the oven to 350 degrees.

Brush the warm peach preserves on the inside of the baked tart shell. Set aside.

For the mango cream, arrange the mango slices on the bottom of the tart shell. Thoroughly beat the egg, egg yolks, light brown sugar, 2 tablespoons granulated sugar, and vanilla in a mixing bowl. Blend in the heavy cream. Pour the custard mixture into the tart shell. Dot the top with the bits of butter and sprinkle the remaining 1 1/2 teaspoons sugar evenly over the top.

Bake the tart on a rack in the lower third of the preheated oven for about 25 minutes, or until the custard is set.

Transfer the tart to a cooling rack. Cool completely. Serve the tart cut into pie-shaped wedges.

# Giant Peach Empanadas

These empanadas are like the essence of summer in a flaky pastry dough. The turnovers are irresistible served warm from the oven with softly whipped cream or vanilla ice cream.

[SERVES 8]

**For the peach filling:**

2 tablespoons cornstarch
½ cup granulated sugar
¼ teaspoon freshly grated
  nutmeg
¼ teaspoon ground cinnamon
Pinch salt

6 large peaches, peeled,
  pitted, cubed, and tossed
  with 2 teaspoons freshly
  squeezed lemon juice
¼ teaspoon pure vanilla
  extract

**For the pastry dough:**

2 sheets pie dough made from
  2 recipes Flaky Pie Crust
  (see pages 31–35), chilled

About 2 tablespoons ice
  water

About 1 tablespoon granulated
  sugar

Lightly butter and flour a large cookie sheet. Set aside. Preheat the oven to 425 degrees.

For the peach filling, thoroughly combine the cornstarch, sugar, nutmeg, cinnamon, and salt in a large mixing bowl. Add the peaches and vanilla and stir well.

For the pastry dough, remove one of the two sheets of pie crust from the refrigerator. Peel off the top sheet of wax paper and cut out a 9-inch circle of dough, trimming away the outer scraps; invert the circle onto a lightly floured wooden board and peel

away the remaining sheet of wax paper. Spoon half of the filling in a mound on one side of the circle, leaving a 1½-inch border. Brush ice water around the border of the dough on the fruit side (leave the other semicircle dry). Fold over the pastry dough to enclose the fruit, pressing the edges so that they stick together. Transfer the empanada to the prepared cookie sheet. Repeat with the remaining circle of dough and filling.

Using a table fork, seal the rounded edge of each turnover by pressing the tines firmly into the dough. Chill for 10 minutes. Brush the top of each empanada with a film of ice water. Sprinkle a little granulated sugar over the top. Cut several steam vents in the top of each empanada with a small, sharp knife.

Bake the empanadas on a rack set in the lower third of the preheated oven for 15 minutes. Reduce the oven temperature to 350 degress and continue baking for 25 to 30 minutes longer, or until the pastry is golden.

Set the cookie sheet on a cooling rack and let stand for 15 minutes. Carefully remove the empanadas with a very wide metal spatula to another cooling rack. When they are completely cooled, transfer to a large, flat plate and slice into sections for serving. Alternately, slice the empanadas directly on the cookie sheet.

# Pear Foldover

In my kitchen, a foldover is sliced, lightly sweetened and spiced fruit piled onto a round or retangular sheet of pie dough; the border of dough is casually folded over part of the filling, leaving a good portion of fruit exposed.

Serve slices of Pear Foldover with softly whipped cream or crème fraîche accented with a dash of maple syrup or liquid brown sugar.

[SERVES 4]

**For the pastry dough:**

>*1 sheet pie dough made from*
>*1 recipe Flaky Pie Crust*
>*(see pages 31–35), chilled*

**For the pears:**

>*4 firm but ripe pears, peeled,*
>*cored, sliced, and tossed*
>*with 2 teaspoons freshly*
>*squeezed lemon juice*
>*2 tablespoons granulated*
>*sugar blended with*
>*1 tablespoon firmly packed*
>*light brown sugar,*
>*3/4 teaspoon ground*
>*cinnamon, and 1/4 teaspoon*
>*freshly grated nutmeg*

>*2 tablespoons chopped lightly*
>*toasted walnuts*
>*3 tablespoons passion fruit*
>*jam, at room temperature*
>*(apricot, peach, or quince*
>*jam may be substituted)*

Lightly butter and flour a cookie sheet. Set aside. Preheat the oven to 375 degrees.

For the pastry dough, remove the sheet of dough from the refrigerator. Peel off the top sheet of wax paper. Carefully invert the

sheet on the buttered and floured cookie sheet. Peel off the second sheet of wax paper. Let the dough stand for about 5 minutes, or until it is no longer rigid from cold storage.

For the pears, thoroughly toss together the pears, sugar-spice blend, and walnuts.

Brush 2 tablespoons of the jam over the surface of the pastry dough, leaving a 2-inch border free of jam. Spoon the pears over the pastry. Gather up the edges in segments with the help of a thin, flexible spatula or palette knife and fold over the fruit; small pleats will be formed around the pastry as you press down the dough. Brush the remaining tablespoon of jam over the top of the fruit.

Bake the foldover on a rack in the lower third of the preheated oven for about 40 to 50 minutes, or until the pastry is golden and the fruit is tender.

Transfer the cookie sheet to a cooling rack. Let stand for 15 minutes. Carefully transfer the foldover to a second cooling rack, using 2 wide metal spatulas. Alternatively, slice the foldover directly on the cookie sheet.

Slice the foldover on the diagonal and serve hot or warm.

*Variation*

Foldovers are good made with sliced apples (use 4 medium-sized tart cooking apples, peeled and sliced) or narrow ripe apricot wedges (use about 12 to 15 small apricots); either is an excellent substitute for pears.

# Apple Dumplings

Serve these oven-fresh dumplings warm, with heavy cream.

[SERVES 4]

2 tablespoons firmly packed
   light brown sugar
¼ teaspoon ground cinnamon
⅛ teaspoon freshly grated
   nutmeg
1 tablespoon unsalted butter,
   softened at room
   temperature
4 small tart cooking apples,
   peeled and cored

1 extra-large egg white,
   beaten until frothy
1 sheet pie dough made from
   1 recipe Flaky Pie Crust
   (see pages 31–35 and Note
   at the end of this recipe)
About 2 tablespoons ice water
About 1 tablespoon granulated
   sugar

Preheat the oven to 425 degrees.

Combine the light brown sugar, cinnamon, nutmeg, and butter in a small bowl. Fill the cored apples with the mixture, dividing it evenly among them.

Brush the egg white over the surface of the pie dough. Cut the dough into 4 squares. Place each apple in the center of a square of dough and fold up the sides to enclose the fruit, pressing the seams together.

Place the dumplings on an ungreased jelly roll pan, spacing them about 3 inches apart. Brush the outside of each dumpling with ice water and dust with sugar.

Bake the dumplings on a rack in the middle of the preheated oven for 10 minutes. Reduce the oven temperature to 350 degrees and continue baking the dumplings for 40 minutes longer, or until the pastry dough is golden and the fruit is tender.

Transfer the pan to a cooling rack. Cool 5 minutes. Carefully remove the dumplings to a second cooling rack, using a wide metal spatula.

*Fruit Desserts*

Serve the dumplings warm or at room temperature.

NOTE: It is helpful to roll the pastry dough for dumplings into a rough square, which can then be cut into 4 even pieces to wrap around the fruit.

*Variation*

For *Pear Dumplings*, substitute 4 firm, ripe pears for the apples. To prepare the pears, peel them, leaving the stems intact. Cut a thin slice off the bottom of each pear, and core. Fill each cavity with some of the sugar and spice mixture, packing it in lightly.

# 3

## Puddings and Shortcakes, Fools and Mousses

Blackberry-Orange Pudding

Raspberry-Chocolate Pudding

Plum Bread Pudding
*Variations: Peach Bread Pudding, Nectarine Bread Pudding*

Spiced Persimmon Pudding

Summer Pudding
*Variation: Summer Fruit Pudding*

Apricot Pudding
*Variations: Prune Pudding, Pear Pudding*

Dried Fruit Clafouti

Apple Clafouti
*Variations: Pear Clafouti, Fresh Fig Clafouti,
Nectarine Clafouti, Cherry Clafouti*

*Strawberry Shortcake*
*Variations: Peach Shortcake, Fresh Raspberry Shortcake,*
*Fresh Blackberry Shortcake*

*Blueberry Shortcake Triangles*

*Raspberry Fool*
*Variations: Strawberry Fool, Apple Fool,*
*Peach Fool, Blackberry Fool, Apricot Fool*

*Lemon Cream Mousse with Blueberries*
*Variation: Lemon Cream Mousse with Raspberries*

*Frozen Peach Mousse*
*Variations: Frozen Nectarine Mousse, Frozen Strawberry Mousse,*
*Frozen Mango Mousse, Frozen Apricot Mousse,*
*Frozen Pear Mousse*

P̲uddings, shortcakes, and fools have a warm, inviting—and sometimes homespun—appearance, and are made of ingredients that are often on hand.

The silky baked puddings in this chapter are based on custard mixtures flavored with chocolate or orange and dotted with raspberries and blackberries, layered with sliced fruit and bread for bread pudding, or poured over dried or sautéed fruit to form a clafouti.

The Blackberry-Orange Pudding and the Raspberry-Chocolate Pudding are old, old recipes that are variations on a familiar nursery-style dessert: Each pudding forms two layers as it bakes, one similar to a sponge cake and the other like a soft stovetop-cooked pudding interspersed with fruit. Both are good served warm or at room temperature, with a side mound of lightly whipped cream. Either sweet can be put together in the time it takes to preheat the oven, resulting in a fine from-scratch dessert baked while you are making a main course.

*Puddings and Shortcakes, Fools and Mousses*

[69]

The Apple Clafouti, with its pear, nectarine, fig, and cherry variations, and the Dried Fruit Clafouti are batter puddings: In each, an egg- and cream-enriched, vanilla-flavored flour mixture is poured over fresh, dried, or sautéed fruit. A clafouti is easy to make and can incorporate a range of seasonal fruit—a cupful of blueberries or blackberries, sliced peaches, or plums.

Shortcake combines three of my favorite things—biscuits, fruit, and cream. The shortcake dough that I am fond of making is tender-textured and sweetened with a bit of granulated sugar. A shortcake dough is quite easy to cut into various shapes (rounds, diamonds, hearts, triangles), or it can be pressed into a round or square pan and baked into one solid cake, then cut into squares or wedges. The fruit, be it berries, sliced peaches, nectarines, or plums, is either treated to a preliminary cooking and served as a warm compote over and about the pieces of shortcake or used in its natural state. In the Blueberry Shortcake Triangles, for example, part of the blueberries is cooked into a chunky sauce, then combined with the remaining uncooked berries. This makes a delectable topping for shortcake.

While we tend to think that shortcake should be made with summer fruit alone, consider pairing the oven-hot biscuits with apples or pears. Apples are lovely sautéed in butter, sugar, and spices, then finished off with a splash of cider or apple brandy. Pears can be sliced and sautéed in the same fashion as apples, or they can be halved and poached in pear nectar or white grape juice with a sprinkling of sugar and a cinnamon stick; cut the warm poached pears into chunks or thick slices, lavish them in between layers of shortcake and top with maple syrup–sweetened whipped cream.

A fruit fool is a light but rich dessert made by combining puréed fruit with whipped cream. Fruit that is fleshy—peaches, nectarines, pears, apples, and plums—makes a slightly firmer fool than one made from cooked whole berries. For berry fools, I sometimes fold

in an extra handful of whole, ripe berries to add a little more fullness to the dessert.

A frozen fruit mousse, consisting of egg yolks, heavy cream, a sugar syrup, and a fruit purée, is an easy sweet to prepare. The mixture can be spooned into one large bowl or individual ramekins, tucked away in the freezer, and used over the next several days.

And remember that it's perfectly fine to use overripe or slightly blemished fruit when you are making a fool or a mousse; just be sure to trim the fruit carefully before it is cooked or processed into a purée.

# Blackberry-Orange Pudding

This lovely recipe comes from my paternal grandmother, Lilly Yockelson, who delighted in turning out blackberry jam and blackberry pies, and whipping up the following pudding.

Here is my version of her old-time recipe, and there are many variations of it in use today. The Raspberry-Chocolate Pudding on page 74 is yet another variation.

[SERVES 6]

*2/3 cup fresh plump blackberries*
*1/4 cup unsifted cake flour*
*3/4 cup plus 2 tablespoons Orange-Scented Granulated Sugar (page 173)*
*Pinch salt*
*3 tablespoons unsalted butter, melted and cooled (or substitute margarine)*
*4 extra-large egg yolks, at room temperature*

*5 tablespoons freshly squeezed orange juice*
*2 teaspoons finely grated orange peel*
*3/4 cup milk, at room temperature*
*1/2 cup light cream, at room temperature*
*3 extra-large egg whites, at room temperature*
*Pinch cream of tartar*
*3 tablespoons superfine sugar*

Lightly butter a 6-cup ovenproof baking dish that measures 2 inches deep. Sprinkle the blackberries on the bottom of the baking dish. Set aside. Preheat the oven to 350 degrees.

Thoroughly combine the flour, orange-scented sugar, and salt in a large mixing bowl. Whisk the butter, egg yolks, orange juice, and orange peel in a small bowl; pour over the flour mixture and blend well. Blend in the milk and light cream. Beat the egg whites until frothy, add the cream of tartar, and continue beating until soft peaks form. Sprinkle over the superfine sugar and beat until

firm (not stiff) peaks form. Stir one quarter of the egg whites into the orange mixture, then fold in the remaining whites. Carefully pour and scrape the batter into the baking dish, directly over the blackberries.

Place the dish of pudding in a baking pan large enough to accommodate it. Pour enough warm water in the pan to rise a little less than halfway up the sides of the baking dish.

Bake the entire assembly on a rack set in the lower third of the preheated oven for 40 to 45 minutes, or until nicely puffed, a light golden color, and set. Carefully remove the pudding dish from the water bath and place it on a cooling rack.

Serve the pudding warm or at room temperature.

BAKING NOTE: Using cake flour in the pudding batter creates a most delicate dessert, I think. My grandmother used all-purpose flour, and that is a highly acceptable substitute.

# Raspberry-Chocolate Pudding

Soft and creamy, this baked pudding separates into two layers as it bakes, forming a custardy bottom under a spongecake top. I have used many kinds of bittersweet chocolate in this dessert—Lindt Excellence or Tobler Tradition gives it the best flavor.

[SERVES 6]

¾ cup firm but ripe red raspberries
2½ ounces (2½ squares) unsweetened chocolate, chopped
1½ ounces (1½ squares or half a 3-ounce bar) semisweet or bittersweet chocolate, chopped
1 cup milk
6 tablespoons light cream
3 tablespoons unsalted butter (or substitute margarine)
¾ cup Vanilla-Scented Granulated Sugar (page 173)

¼ cup plus 1½ teaspoons unsifted all-purpose flour
Pinch salt
4 extra-large egg yolks, at room temperature
2 teaspoons pure vanilla extract
1 teaspoon chocolate extract
3 extra-large egg whites, at room temperature
3 tablespoons superfine sugar
Whipped cream (optional)

Lightly butter a 6-cup ovenproof baking dish that measures 2 inches deep. Sprinkle the raspberries on the bottom of the dish. Set aside. Preheat the oven to 350 degrees.

Place both kinds of chocolate, milk, cream, and butter in a medium-sized saucepan set over low heat, and cook, stirring occasionally, until the chocolate has melted completely. Remove from the heat and set aside to cool slightly.

Thoroughly combine the granulated sugar, flour, and salt in a

large mixing bowl. Whisk in the chocolate-milk mixture, egg yolks, vanilla, and chocolate extract, mixing thoroughly to form a smooth batter.

Beat the egg whites in a bowl until soft peaks form; add the superfine sugar and continue beating until firm (not stiff) peaks form. Stir one quarter of the egg whites into the chocolate mixture, then fold in the remaining whites. Carefully pour and scrape the batter into the prepared baking dish, directly over the raspberries.

Place the dish of pudding in a baking pan large enough to accommodate it. Pour enough warm water in the pan to rise a little less than halfway up the sides of the baking dish.

Bake the entire assembly on a rack set in the lower third of the preheated oven for 40 to 45 minutes, or until nicely puffed and set. Carefully remove the pudding dish from the water bath and place it on a cooling rack.

Serve the pudding warm or at room temperature, accompanied by spoonfuls of lightly sweetened whipped cream, if you like.

*Puddings and Shortcakes, Fools and Mousses*

# Plum Bread Pudding

Custardy and, as desserts go, hearty, bread pudding is a triumph of simple dairy ingredients and good-quality bread.

[SERVES 8]

4 tablespoons (½ stick) unsalted butter, at room temperature (or substitute margarine)

Eight to ten ½- to ¾-inch-thick slices of homestyle white bread, egg bread (challah), or brioche, crusts removed

4 firm but ripe red plums, halved, pitted, sliced, and well drained on sheets of paper towels

3 extra-large eggs, at room temperature

3 extra-large egg yolks, at room temperature

¾ cup superfine sugar blended with ½ teaspoon ground cinnamon and ¼ teaspoon freshly grated nutmeg

2½ cups milk, at room temperature

1 cup heavy cream, at room temperature

½ cup light cream, at room temperature

Pinch salt

2 teaspoons pure vanilla extract

Confectioners' sugar (optional)

Lightly butter a 2-quart (12- to 14-inch) ovenproof baking dish measuring about 2¾ to 3 inches deep. Set aside. Preheat the oven to 350 degrees.

Lightly butter the slices of bread on one side, using the 4 tablespoons of butter. Cut each slice of bread in half on the diagonal, forming two triangles; arrange the triangles, buttered side down, on the bottom of the baking dish. Scatter the plum slices over and between the slices of bread.

Beat the eggs, egg yolks, and sugar-spice blend in a large mixing bowl for 3 or 4 minutes, or until well blended. Whisk in the milk, heavy cream, and light cream. Blend in the salt and vanilla. Strain

the mixture over the bread. Let stand for 30 minutes.

Place the dish of pudding in a baking dish large enough to accommodate it. Pour enough warm water in the pan to rise a little less than halfway up the sides of the dish holding the pudding.

Bake the entire assembly on a rack in the lower third of the preheated oven for about 40 to 50 minutes, or until just set (a knife inserted 2 inches from the edge will emerge without any moist particles clinging to it).

Carefully remove the pudding dish from the water bath and place it on a cooling rack. Cut the pudding into squares and serve warm or at room temperature, sprinkled with a little confectioners' sugar, if you like.

*Variations*

For *Peach Bread Pudding*, substitute for the plums 3 ripe peaches, peeled, halved, pitted, sliced, and drained on paper towels.

For *Nectarine Bread Pudding*, substitute for the plums 3 ripe nectarines, halved, pitted, sliced, and drained on paper towels.

# Spiced Persimmon Pudding

The quartet of spices used in this recipe—cinnamon, nutmeg, ginger, and allspice—are those that flavor most harvest fruits and vegetables, such as pumpkin, hubbard and acorn squash, sweet potatoes, pears, and apples.

Spiced Persimmon Pudding is delicious served as is, or with dabs of hard sauce, a warm lemon sauce, or lightly whipped heavy cream sweetened with a touch of maple syrup.

[SERVES 6]

5 or 6 very ripe persimmons, or enough to yield 2 cups persimmon purée
1 teaspoon finely grated orange peel
1/4 cup freshly squeezed orange juice
3/4 cup unsifted cake flour
1/2 teaspoon baking powder
1/2 teaspoon baking soda
3/4 teaspoon ground cinnamon
1/2 teaspoon freshly grated nutmeg
1/4 teaspoon ground ginger
Pinch ground allspice
2 extra-large eggs, separated, at room temperature

2 extra-large egg yolks, at room temperature
Pinch salt
3/4 cup superfine sugar
7 tablespoons unsalted butter, melted and cooled (or substitute margarine)
1 cup milk, at room temperature
1 cup heavy cream, at room temperature
1 tablespoon light rum
1 teaspoon pure vanilla extract

Lightly butter an 8-cup ovenproof baking dish that measures 2 inches deep. Set aside. Preheat the oven to 350 degrees.

Peel the persimmons and scrape away the flesh from the filaments that compose the central core. Purée the flesh in the container of a food processor fitted with the steel blade, or through a

food mill fitted with the medium disk. Turn the purée into a bowl; stir in the orange peel and orange juice. Set aside.

Sift the cake flour with the baking powder, baking soda, cinnamon, nutmeg, ginger, and allspice onto a sheet of wax paper. Beat the 4 egg yolks with the salt and sugar in a large mixing bowl. Blend in the butter and persimmon purée. Stir in the sifted mixture, mixing well. Stir in the milk, a little at a time; stir in the heavy cream, a little at a time. Blend in the rum and vanilla.

Beat the egg whites in a bowl until firm (not stiff) peaks form. Stir a big spoonful of the whites into the pudding mixture, then fold in the remaining whites. Pour and scrape the batter into the prepared baking dish.

Bake the pudding on a rack in the lower third of the preheated oven for about 40 minutes, or until set and just firm to the touch.

Transfer the pudding to a cooling rack. Serve warm or at room temperature.

# Summer Pudding

In this English pudding, cooked and sweetened blueberries, strawberries, and raspberries are spooned into a bread-lined bowl and refrigerated. The fruit juice is absorbed into the bread and tints it.

[SERVES 5]

1½ cups blueberries, picked over

1 cup strawberries, hulled and halved if large

½ cup ripe red, black, or golden raspberries

½ cup blackberries, picked over

½ cup plus 2 tablespoons Lemon-Scented Granulated Sugar (page 173), or to more to taste

1 teaspoon freshly squeezed lemon juice

5 tablespoons apple juice

6 to 8 slices good-quality, homestyle white bread, trimmed of crusts, or more as needed

1 cup cold heavy cream

For the pudding, place the blueberries, strawberries, raspberries, blackberries, sugar, lemon juice, and apple juice in a large, heavy, nonreactive saucepan or casserole. Cover, place over moderate heat, and cook for 7 or 8 minutes, or until the juice from the berries has welled up considerably. Remove from the heat and let stand uncovered.

While the berries are cooking, line a 4- to 5-cup bowl or straight-sided casserole with the slices of bread: Trim one slice to fit the bottom, then cut and fit the other slices around the sides of the dish. Plug in any small open gaps with extra pieces of bread.

Spoon the warm berry mixture into the bread-lined dish. Cover the top of the pudding with a slice of bread and fill in any open

spaces with smaller pieces of bread. Cover the top with a sheet of plastic wrap.

Set the pudding dish in a large, wide bowl or nonreactive baking dish. Place a small plate right on top of the pudding. (The plate should be slightly smaller than the circumference of the pudding dish.) Weigh down the plate by putting something heavy on top (I use a 15-ounce can of tomatoes). Refrigerate the pudding for at least 8 hours, or overnight.

Remove the weight, saucer, and plastic wrap from the pudding. Gently loosen the pudding by easing a flexible palette knife or very thin spatula between the bread and bowl. Place a deep serving dish on top of the pudding. Carefully invert the pudding and remove the bowl or casserole. Alternatively, just serve the pudding directly from the bowl.

Whip the cream until soft peaks form.

Serve portions of the pudding with dollops of the whipped cream.

*Variation*

To make a *Summer Fruit Pudding* use 3½ cups of a combination of summer fruits, such as diced peaches or nectarines, halved and pitted cherries, blueberries, raspberries (red or golden), blackberries, and thickly sliced strawberries. The fruit may be cooked with 1 cinnamon stick and plain granulated sugar, if you like.

# Apricot Pudding

This is an old-fashioned dessert that combines the best qualities of a cake and a pudding.

Serve the pudding warm or at room temperature, with whipped cream or heavy cream.

[SERVES 5 OR 6]

½ cup (about 3 ounces) dried apricots
½ cup unsifted all-purpose flour
½ cup unsifted cake flour
½ teaspoon baking soda
Pinch salt
½ teaspoon ground cinnamon
¼ teaspoon freshly grated nutmeg
6 tablespoons unsalted butter, softened at room temperature (or substitute margarine)

2 tablespoons shortening
⅓ cup Vanilla-Scented Superfine Sugar (page 173), or plain superfine sugar
2 extra-large eggs, at room temperature
1 teaspoon pure vanilla extract
½ cup sour cream, at room temperature

For the spiced coconut topping:

1 tablespoon granulated sugar
¼ teaspoon ground cinnamon
¼ cup loosely packed sweetened flaked coconut

1 tablespoon cold unsalted butter, cut into bits (or substitute margarine)

Lightly butter a 12-inch round or oval baking dish that measures 1¾ inches high. Set aside. Preheat the oven to 350 degrees.

Place the apricots in a bowl, cover with hot water, and set aside

for 15 minutes for the fruit to plump up; drain the apricots well, then coarsely chop. Set aside.

Sift the all-purpose flour and cake flour with the baking soda, salt, cinnamon, and nutmeg onto a sheet of wax paper. Cream the butter and shortening in the large bowl of an electric mixer on moderately high speed for 3 minutes. Add the sugar and continue beating for 1 or 2 minutes longer. Beat in the eggs, one at a time, blending well after each addition. Beat in the vanilla extract and sour cream. On low speed, add the sifted mixture and beat just until the particles of flour have been absorbed. Fold in the chopped apricots and spoon the batter into the prepared pan.

For the topping, combine the sugar, cinnamon, and coconut in a small bowl. Sprinkle the mixture evenly over the top of the batter. Dot the top of the pudding with the bits of butter.

Bake the pudding on a rack set in the middle of the preheated oven for 30 minutes, or until golden and a wooden pick inserted into the cake withdraws clean and dry.

Transfer the pudding to a cooling rack. Serve warm or at room temperature.

*Variations*

For *Prune Pudding*, substitute for the apricots ¾ cup (about 5 ounces) pitted prunes. Plump the prunes in hot water or hot tea for 15 minutes, drain well, and pat dry on paper towels.

For *Pear Pudding*, substitute for the apricots 5 canned pears halves (packed in natural juices), well drained and thickly sliced, omitting the soaking. Spoon the batter into the pan, scatter the pear slices on top of the batter, and sprinkle over the topping.

# Dried Fruit Clafouti

This clafouti, made with a mixture of dried fruit plumped in hot cider, is a good wintertime dessert. Although I have specified a particular mixture of dried fruit, you could certainly use up any odd lots of fruit you have in the pantry, as long as there is some variety.

[SERVES 6]

1 tablespoon unsalted butter, softened at room temperature (or substitute margarine)

1/4 cup (about 2 ounces) dried cherries

5 (about 1 ounce) dried apricot halves

5 (about 2 ounces) dried peach halves

4 (about 3 ounces) dried figs, stemmed

4 (about 2 ounces) pitted prunes

2 tablespoons (about 3/4 ounce) dark seedless raisins

1 cup apple cider, heated to boiling

1/2 cup Vanilla-Scented Superfine Sugar (page 173), or substitute plain superfine sugar

2 extra-large eggs, at room temperature

2 extra-large egg yolks, at room temperature

1/4 teaspoon ground allspice

1/4 teaspoon freshly grated nutmeg

1/4 teaspoon ground ginger

Pinch salt

3/4 teaspoon pure almond extract

1/4 teaspoon pure vanilla extract

1/2 cup unsifted all-purpose flour

2 tablespoons unsifted cake flour

1 1/3 cups milk, at room temperature

3 tablespoons heavy cream, at room temperature

Confectioners' sugar

Whipped cream or crème fraîche (optional)

Preheat the oven to 375 degrees. Smear the 1 tablespoon butter on the bottom of a 6-cup ovenproof baking dish measuring about 2 inches deep. Set aside.

Place the cherries, apricots, peaches, figs, prunes, and raisins in a large heatproof bowl. Pour over the hot cider, stir, and let the fruit stand for about 30 minutes, or until plumped. Drain the fruit from the cider and pat dry on sheets of paper towels. Coarsely chop the apricots, peaches, figs, and prunes and scatter them, along with the cherries and raisins, on the bottom of the buttered baking dish.

Place the sugar, eggs, egg yolks, allspice, nutmeg, ginger, salt, almond extract, vanilla extract, all-purpose flour, cake flour, milk, and heavy cream in the container of a food processor fitted with the steel blade or in the container of a blender, and cover. If using a food processor, process the ingredients just until a batter is formed, scrape down the sides of the work bowl, and process again for a few seconds; if using a blender, blend on high speed for 45 seconds to 1 minute until a smooth batter is formed.

Pour the batter over the dried fruit. Bake the clafouti on a rack in the middle of the preheated oven for 15 minutes, reduce the oven temperature to 350 degrees, and continue baking for 20 minutes longer, or until puffed and set.

Transfer the clafouti to a cooling rack. Let stand for 3 or 4 minutes. Sift confectioners' sugar generously over the top. Spoon portions of clafouti onto dessert plates and serve immediately with lightly sweetened whipped cream or crème fraîche, if you like.

# Apple Clafouti

The clafouti emerges from the oven all puffed and golden, and is wonderful eaten right away, with plenty of confectioners' sugar sifted over the top. The egg-enriched batter is child's play to make in a blender or food processor.

[SERVES 6]

1 tablespoon unsalted butter (or substitute margarine)
2 firm, crisp cooking apples, peeled, halved, cored, and cut into ⅓-inch-thick slices
1 tablespoon firmly packed brown sugar
1 tablespoon bourbon, or apple cider or apple juice
2 extra-large eggs, at room temperature
2 extra-large egg yolks, at room temperature
½ cup superfine sugar
Pinch salt
¼ teaspoon ground cinnamon
¼ teaspoon freshly grated nutmeg

1½ teaspoons pure vanilla extract
Seed scrapings from the inside of half a vanilla bean
½ cup unsifted all-purpose flour
2 tablespoons unsifted cake flour
1⅓ cups milk, at room temperature
3 tablespoons heavy cream, at room temperature
Confectioners' sugar
Whipped cream or crème fraîche (optional)

Preheat the oven to 375 degrees.

Put the butter in a skillet and place over moderately high heat; when the butter has melted, add the apple slices and stir-cook for 1 minute. Sprinkle over the brown sugar and stir-cook for 2 minutes. Add the bourbon and stir-cook for 1 minute longer, or until the apple slices are barely tender.

Turn the apple slices, with all of the cooking juices, into a

*Fruit Desserts*

lightly buttered 6-cup ovenproof baking dish about 2 inches deep. Set aside.

Place the eggs, egg yolks, superfine sugar, salt, cinnamon, nutmeg, vanilla, seed scrapings from the vanilla bean, all-purpose flour, cake flour, milk, and heavy cream in the container of a food processor fitted with the steel blade or in the container of a blender, and cover. If using a food processor, process the ingredients just until a batter is formed; scrape down the sides of the work bowl and process again for a second or two longer; if using a blender, blend on high speed for 45 seconds to 1 minute, or until a smooth batter is formed.

Pour the pudding batter over the apples. Bake the clafouti on a rack in the middle of the preheated oven for 15 minutes, reduce the oven temperature to 350 degrees, and continue baking for 20 minutes longer, or until puffed and set.

Transfer the clafouti to a cooling rack. Let stand for 3 or 4 minutes. Sift confectioners' sugar generously over the top. Spoon portions of clafouti onto dessert plates and serve immediately with lightly sweetened whipped cream or crème fraîche, if you like.

### Variations

To make a *Pear Clafouti*, substitute 2 firm, ripe pears, peeled, cored, and sliced, for the apple. Sprinkle 1 tablespoon moist dried currants over the sautéed pears. Pour on the batter and bake as directed.

To make a *Fresh Fig Clafouti*, substitute 6 firm, ripe purple figs for the apple. Stem the figs and cut each into 4 to 6 wedges. Omit the brown sugar and bourbon. Instead, smear the bottom of the 6-cup baking dish with 1 tablespoon softened unsalted butter and scatter over the fig sections. Pour on the batter and bake as directed.
(continued)

To make a *Nectarine Clafouti*, substitute 2 ripe nectarines, peeled, pitted, and sliced, for the apple. Omit the brown sugar and bourbon. Instead, smear the bottom of the 6-cup baking dish with 1 tablespoon softened unsalted butter and scatter over the nectarine slices. Pour on the batter and bake as directed.

To make a *Cherry Clafouti*, substitute 1 cup halved and pitted sweet Bing cherries for the apple. Omit the brown sugar and bourbon. Instead, smear the bottom of the 6-cup baking dish with 1 tablespoon softened unsalted butter and scatter over the cherries. Pour on the batter and bake as directed.

NOTE: Over the years, I have made many versions of the batter that gets poured over the fresh fruit, and always seem to go back to my oldest recipe, which is the one you have here. But for a less egg yolk–rich clafouti, use 3 extra-large eggs instead of 2 extra-large eggs and 2 extra-large egg yolks.

# Strawberry Shortcake

These biscuits are flecked with the seed scrapings from a vanilla bean, and the berries, some lightly crushed, are sweetened with a little honey or fresh strawberry syrup.

[SERVES 6]

**For the shortcake:**

1¾ cups unsifted all-purpose
  flour
¼ cup unsifted cake flour
1 tablespoon baking powder
¼ teaspoon salt
Seed scrapings from the inside
  of half a split vanilla bean
5 tablespoons cold solid
  shortening

3 tablespoons cold unsalted
  butter, cut into chunks
  (or substitute margarine)
1 tablespoon superfine sugar
¾ cup less 1 tablespoon milk
  blended with ½ teaspoon
  pure vanilla extract, at
  room temperature

**For the strawberries:**

3 cups red, ripe strawberries,
  hulled
3 tablespoons honey

2 teaspoons freshly squeezed
  lemon juice

**For the cream:**

1 cup cold heavy cream
2 tablespoons sifted
  confectioners' sugar

¼ teaspoon pure vanilla
  extract

Small sprigs of fresh mint
(optional)

(continued)

*Puddings and Shortcakes, Fools and Mousses*

Preheat the oven to 425 degrees.

Sift together the all-purpose flour, cake flour, baking powder, and salt into a large mixing bowl. Stir in the vanilla bean seeds. Add the chunks of shortening and butter and, using 2 round-bladed knives, cut the fat into the flour until it is reduced to small, pea-sized bits. With your fingertips, further reduce the fat to small flakes by dipping down into the mixture and crumbling it. Stir in the superfine sugar. Pour over the milk-vanilla blend and stir it in with a few swift strokes. Turn out the dough onto a lightly floured wooden board, knead lightly 5 times, and pat into a cake about ¾ inch thick. Cut out rounds, using a lightly floured 2- to 2½-inch plain round cutter. (There should be about 12 rounds.) Place the rounds on an ungreased cookie sheet, spacing them about 2 inches apart.

Bake the shortcake on a rack set in the lower third of the preheated oven for about 12 to 14 minutes, or until well risen, golden, and firm to the touch.

While the shortcake is baking, place 1 cup of the strawberries in a large mixing bowl; crush with a potato masher or the back of a spoon. Add the remaining 2 cups berries. Stir in the honey and lemon juice; set aside for 10 minutes.

Whip the cream until it just begins to mound, blend in the confectioners' sugar and vanilla, and continue to beat until soft peaks form. Refrigerate the whipped cream.

Remove the cookie sheet from the oven and place on a wire cooling rack. Transfer the rounds to a second cooling rack, using a wide metal spatula.

Split each shortcake in half horizontally with a serrated knife. For each serving, place 2 shortcake rounds on each dessert plate. Sandwich a spoonful of the sweetened strawberries in the middle of each split round and top with a spoonful of the whipped cream and a mint sprig. Serve immediately.

*Variations*

For *Peach Shortcake*, omit the strawberries and honey. Peel, halve, pit, and thickly slice 5 ripe peaches. Toss the peach slices with the lemon juice and 1 tablespoon superfine sugar, or more to taste. Use the peaches in the same way as the strawberries. Five ripe nectarines, halved, pitted, and sliced may be substituted for the peaches.

For *Fresh Raspberry Shortcake*, omit the strawberries, honey, and lemon juice. Pick over 2 cups ripe red, black, or golden raspberries. Carefully toss the raspberries with 2 teaspoons superfine sugar and 2 tablespoons apple juice or black currant liqueur (crème de cassis). Let the raspberries stand for 20 minutes. Use the raspberries in the same way as the strawberries.

For *Fresh Blackberry Shortcake*, omit the strawberries, honey, and lemon juice. Pick over 2 cups firm blackberries. Carefully toss the blackberries with 2 tablespoons superfine sugar (or more to taste, if the blackberries are particularly tart) and 3 tablespoons apple juice. Let stand for 20 minutes. Use the blackberries in the same way as the strawberries.

*Puddings and Shortcakes, Fools and Mousses*

# Blueberry Shortcake Triangles

In this recipe, the filling is a sauce made up of fresh and cooked blueberries. Apart from serving with shortcake, the blueberry compote is an excellent topping for ice cream, slices of pound cake, or bread pudding.

Shortcake is traditionally made with plump split biscuits. But sometimes, to vary the look of shortcake (and if I am in too much of a hurry to stamp out rounds of dough), I bake a softer biscuit dough in a plain 8-inch round baking pan, cut the baked "cake" into triangles, top with fruit, and finish with whipped cream.

[SERVES 6]

**For the shortcake triangles:**

1¾ cups unsifted all-purpose flour
¼ cup unsifted cake flour
1 tablespoon baking powder
¼ teaspoon salt
¼ teaspoon freshly grated nutmeg
¼ teaspoon ground cinnamon
5 tablespoons cold solid shortening

3 tablespoons cold unsalted butter, cut into chunks (or substitute margarine)
1½ tablespoons superfine sugar
1 cup milk blended with 1 teaspoon pure vanilla extract, at room temperature

**For the blueberry compote:**

3 tablespoons granulated sugar (or more to taste) blended with ¼ teaspoon ground cinnamon
2 teaspoons freshly squeezed lemon juice

1 teaspoon finely grated lemon peel
2 cups blueberries, picked over

*Fruit Desserts*

**For the spiced cream:**

*1 cup cold heavy cream*

*2 tablespoons sifted confectioners' sugar blended with ¼ teaspoon ground cinnamon and ⅛ teaspoon freshly grated nutmeg*

For the shortcake, lightly butter and flour the inside of a plain 8-inch round cake pan. Set aside. Preheat the oven to 425 degrees.

Sift together the all-purpose flour, cake flour, baking powder, salt, nutmeg, and cinnamon into a large mixing bowl. Add the chunks of shortening and butter, and using 2 round-bladed knives, cut the fat into the flour until it is reduced to pea-sized bits. With your fingertips, further reduce the fat to small flakes by dipping down into the mixture and crumbling it. Stir in the superfine sugar. Pour over the milk-vanilla mixture and stir it in using a few swift strokes. Turn the dough into the prepared pan, smoothing it out into an even layer.

Bake the shortcake on a rack in the lower third of the preheated oven for about 15 minutes, or until it is golden and firm to the touch. (The shortcake will begin to pull away slightly from sides of the cake pan.)

While the shortcake is baking, place the granulated sugar–cinnamon blend, lemon juice, lemon peel, and 1 cup of the blueberries in a medium-sized nonreactive saucepan. Cover, set over low heat, and cook until the sugar dissolves completely. Raise the heat to moderately high and cook, uncovered, for 1 minute longer. Remove from the heat and spoon the berry mixture into a bowl. Cool for 10 minutes. Stir in the remaining 1 cup of blueberries.

For the spiced cream, whip the cream until it just begins to mound, blend in the spiced confectioners' sugar, and continue to beat until very soft peaks form. Refrigerate the whipped cream.

*(continued)*

*Puddings and Shortcakes, Fools and Mousses*

Remove the baked shortcake from the oven and place on a wire cooling rack; let cool for 2 minutes. Run a thin flexible palette knife around the inside edge of the pan, then invert the shortcake onto a second cooling rack. Invert again so that the shortcake sits right side up.

Cut the shortcake into 6 triangles with a serrated knife. For each portion, halve each triangle horizontally. Transfer each triangle to a plate. Sandwich a big ladleful of the blueberry sauce in between the two triangle layers, then top with a spoonful of the spiced whipped cream. Serve immediately.

*Fruit Desserts*

# Raspberry Fool

This raspberry fool, made from fresh raspberry purée and whipped cream, is light and creamy. The purée may be made up several days in advance and stored in the refrigerator. Other summer berries, such as blueberries, blackberries, huckleberries, and strawberries may be substituted for the raspberries; blackberries, though, are often tart, so count on adding a few more tablespoons of superfine sugar.

[SERVES 5]

2 cups red strawberries, picked over
3 tablespoons superfine sugar
2 tablespoons water
1¼ cups cold heavy cream

3 tablespoons sifted confectioners' sugar
½ teaspoon pure vanilla extract

Place 1¼ cups of the raspberries, the superfine sugar, and water in a small nonreactive casserole; cover, place over low heat, and cook until the sugar dissolves completely. Stir now and then. Cook the berries for about 10 minutes longer, or until they have softened. Uncover the pot and continue cooking for 1 minute longer. Remove from the heat and cool completely. Purée the raspberries, along with any juices, through a food mill fitted with the fine disk. Transfer the purée to a storage container, cover, and refrigerate until very cold, 6 to 8 hours.

Whip the heavy cream until it just begins to mound, add the confectioners' sugar and vanilla, and continue beating until firm peaks form. Pour the raspberry purée into a large bowl and stir in about ½ cup of the whipped cream. Fold in the remaining heavy cream with the remaining ¾ cup whole raspberries.

Pile the fool into individual parfait glasses, flutes, or goblets. Chill for 1 hour before serving.

(continued)

## Variations

For *Strawberry Fool*, substitute for the raspberries 1 cup strawberries, hulled. Purée the uncooked berries in the container of a blender with the superfine sugar (omitting the water); strain through a fine-mesh sieve. Fold the strawberry purée into the sweetened whipped cream. Omit the final fold-through of fruit. Chill and serve.

For *Apple Fool*, omit the raspberries, sugar, and water. Fold 1 cup thick, cold Applesauce (page 22) into the sweetened whipped cream. Omit the final fold-through of fruit. Chill and serve.

For *Peach Fool*, substitute for the raspberries 3 large ripe peaches, peeled, halved, pitted, and cut into chunks. Purée the uncooked peaches in the container of a blender with the sugar (omitting the water). Fold the peach purée into the sweetened whipped cream. Omit the final fold-through of fruit. Chill and serve. Nectarines may be substituted for the peaches.

For *Blackberry Fool*, substitute for the raspberries 1⅓ cups blackberries and increase the amount of superfine sugar to 5 tablespoons or more, to taste. Fold the simmered and chilled blackberry purée into the sweetened whipped cream. Omit the final fold-through of fruit. Chill and serve.

For *Apricot Fool*, substitute for the raspberries one 1-pound can apricots packed in natural juices, drained well, using 1 tablespoon superfine sugar and omitting the water. Purée the apricots with 1 tablespoon of the packing juice and sugar in the container of a blender or in the bowl of a food processor fitted with the steel blade. Fold the apricot purée into the whipped cream. Omit the final fold-through of fruit. Chill and serve.

# Lemon Cream Mousse with Blueberries

This mousse is simply a soft lemon pudding lightened with whipped cream and dotted with berries. The lemon cream is easy to make and can be stored in the refrigerator for several days, ready for a final fold-through of cream and berries.

[SERVES 6]

1 recipe cold lemon cream     1 cup cold heavy cream
  (page 52)                  1 cup blueberries, picked over

Place the chilled lemon cream in a large nonreactive bowl. Whip the cream in another bowl until soft peaks form. Stir 2 or 3 large spoonfuls of the whipped cream into the lemon cream to lighten it, then fold in the remaining cream along with the blueberries.

Spoon the mousse into one large bowl, or individual bowls or goblets. Chill the mousse for at least 20 minutes before serving. (The mousse can be made up to 6 hours in advance; refrigerate loosely covered.)

NOTE: To store the lemon cream, spoon the hot cream into a container as soon as you have added the butter. Immediately press a sheet of plastic wrap directly over the surface of the cream to prevent a skin from forming. When cool, cover tightly, and refrigerate.

## Variation

For *Lemon Cream Mousse with Raspberries,* substitute 1 cup firm, red raspberries for the blueberries. As raspberries are fragile, plan on serving the mousse after the 20-minute chill in the refrigerator.

*Puddings and Shortcakes, Fools and Mousses*

# Frozen Peach Mousse

This mousse is made from simple ingredients: egg yolks, sugar, cream, and a fresh peach purée. To make the purée, peel, halve, and pit 3 large, ripe peaches; cut the fruit into chunks and process in the bowl of a food processor fitted with the steel blade. Other purées, such as nectarine, mango, or strawberry, are made in the same way. Apricots or pears, canned in natural juices and drained, can also be puréed to form a delicious fruit base.

Cooling spoonfuls of this mousse are delicious served with thin butter wafers.

[SERVES 6]

*½ cup granulated sugar*
*4 extra-large egg yolks, at*
   *room temperature*
*1½ cups light cream, scalded*

*1 teaspoon pure vanilla*
   *extract*
*1 cup fresh peach purée*
*¾ cup cold heavy cream*

Whisk the sugar and egg yolks in a heavy saucepan (preferably enameled cast iron). Slowly stir in the scalded cream, set the pan over low heat, and cook, stirring, until the mixture thickens, coats the back of a wooden spoon, and registers 175 degrees on a candy thermometer. Remove from the heat and stir in the vanilla extract. Pour the custard mixture into a bowl, place a piece of plastic wrap directly over the top, and cool completely. Refrigerate the custard mixture, covered, until well chilled, about 8 hours. (The custard can be made up to 1 day in advance.)

Stir the peach purée into the custard mixture. Whip the cream until firm peaks form. Stir a large spoonful of the whipped cream into the fruit mixture, then fold in the remaining cream.

Pour the mousse mixture into a freezerproof bowl, cover tightly, and place in the freezer to firm up, about 8 hours. (The mousse may be prepared up to 4 days in advance.) Alternatively, the

*Fruit Desserts*

mousse may be spooned into individual bowls or ramekins and frozen; smaller portions will firm up in about 1 hour and 15 minutes.

*Variations*

For *Frozen Nectarine Mousse,* substitute for the peach purée 1 cup nectarine purée.

For *Frozen Strawberry Mousse,* substitute for the peach purée 1 cup strawberry purée (made from puréeing 2 cups hulled strawberries).

For *Frozen Mango Mousse,* substitute for the peach purée 1 cup mango purée (made from 2 large mangoes, peeled, flesh scraped from center fibrous pit, and puréed).

For *Frozen Apricot Mousse,* substitute for the peach purée 1 cup apricot purée (made from one 16-ounce can apricots in natural juices, drained well and puréed).

For *Frozen Pear Mousse,* substitute for the peach purée 1 cup pear purée (made from one 16-ounce can pears in natural juices, drained well and puréed).

# 4

# Cobblers
# and Crisps

Apple Cobbler

Peach Cobbler

Blueberry Crisp

Cherry-Almond Crisp

Three-Berry Crisp

Rhubarb Crisp

Cranberry-Pear Crisp

Gingered Pear Crisp

Pineapple-Macadamia Crisp

Apple Brown Betty

Cobblers and crisps consist of a single layer of fruit sheltered by a topping. The fruit is sweetened and spiced, and sometimes buttered or lightly thickened. Toppings may take the form of a soft biscuit dough, rolled biscuit dough, or a crumble made up of nuts, sugar, butter, brown sugar, or shredded macaroons (or other kinds of cookies).

In *The Dictionary of American Food and Drink* (New Haven and New York: Ticknor and Fields, 1983), author John F. Mariani describes a cobbler as "a western deep-dish pie with a thick crust and a fruit filling." Traditionally, the top of a cobbler is made up of round biscuits that, when baked, resemble cobblestones, although a softer drop biscuit covering appears in many recipes, old and new, as does a pastry covering. A crisp is a pudding consisting of a thick layer of fruit and a toss of flour, butter, sugar, spices and, most times, nuts. Occasionally, you will come upon a crisp made up of leftover cake crumbs or crumbled cookies, plus butter and spices.

To prepare whole fruit for any of the two-layer desserts, peel, core, pit (if necessary), and cut the fruit into ½-inch-thick slices. Berries need only be picked over for stems and leaves. After tossing the slices with the sweetener called for in the particular recipe, let the fruit stand for a few minutes—in either the baking dish or the mixing bowl—until some of the juices begin to trickle out; this makes for a more flavorful dessert.

Served forth warm from the oven, cobblers and crisps are fragrant and inviting. Anything creamy, such as scoops of ice cream, a light custard sauce, or whipped cream, is an excellent companion. And just before serving, any of the cobblers can be topped with a haze of confectioners' sugar.

## Apple Cobbler

A warm apple cobbler, served with vanilla ice cream or heavy cream, is one of the joys of the fall dessert kitchen.

[SERVES 5 TO 6]

**For the apples:**

6 large tart cooking apples,
peeled, cored, and sliced

1/4 cup granulated sugar, or
more to taste, blended with
3/4 teaspoon ground
cinnamon, 1/4 teaspoon
freshly grated nutmeg, and
1/8 teaspoon ground cloves

2 teaspoons freshly squeezed
lemon juice

2 tablespoons apple cider, or
apple juice

1 tablespoon golden raisins

2 tablespoons unsalted butter,
melted (or substitute
margarine)

**For the cobbler topping:**

1¾ cups unsifted all-purpose
  flour
¼ cup unsifted cake flour
1 tablespoon baking powder
½ teaspoon salt
½ teaspoon freshly grated
  nutmeg
½ teaspoon ground cinnamon

¼ teaspoon ground allspice
8 tablespoons cold solid
  shortening
2 tablespoons plus 2 teaspoons
  granulated sugar
⅔ cup light cream, at room
  temperature

Lightly butter an 8-cup ovenproof baking dish that measures about 2 inches deep. Set aside. Preheat the oven to 425 degrees.

Toss the sliced apples with the sugar-spice blend, lemon juice, apple cider, and raisins. Spoon the apples into the buttered baking dish. Drizzle over the melted butter.

For the cobbler topping, sift the all-purpose flour, cake flour, baking powder, salt, nutmeg, cinnamon, and allspice into a large mixing bowl. Add the chunks of shortening and, using 2 round-bladed knives, cut the fat into the flour until it is reduced to small bits. With your fingertips, further reduce the fat to small flakes by dipping down into the mixture and crumbling it. Stir in 2 table-spoons granulated sugar. Pour over the cream mixture and stir it in with a few brief strokes.

Turn out the dough onto a lightly floured work surface, knead 5 times, and pat it to a thickness of about ¾ inch. Cut biscuits from the dough, using a plain 2½- to 3-inch round biscuit cutter. Place the biscuits on top of the fruit, overlapping them slightly. Sprinkle the remaining 2 teaspoons granulated sugar on top of the biscuits.

Bake the cobbler on a rack in the lower third of the preheated oven for 15 minutes. Reduce the oven temperature to 400 degrees and continue baking for 20 to 25 minutes longer, or until the topping is golden and the fruit is bubbly and tender.

Serve the cobbler warm or at room temperature.

# Peach Cobbler

Warm helpings of peach cobbler are delicious served with heavy cream or vanilla ice cream.

[SERVES 5 TO 6]

**For the peaches:**

6 large peaches, peeled, halved, pitted, and sliced

¹/₄ cup granulated sugar blended with 1 tablespoon cornstarch, ¹/₄ teaspoon freshly grated nutmeg, and ¹/₄ teaspoon ground cinnamon

**For the cobbler topping:**

2 cups unsifted all-purpose flour

1 tablespoon baking powder

¹/₄ teaspoon salt

4 tablespoons (¹/₂ stick) cold unsalted butter, cut into chunks (or substitute margarine)

4 tablespoons cold solid shortening

2 tablespoons plus 2 teaspoons granulated sugar

²/₃ cup plus 1 tablespoon heavy cream blended with 1 teaspoon pure vanilla extract, at room temperature

Lightly butter an 8-cup ovenproof baking dish that measures about 2 inches deep. Set aside. Preheat the oven to 425 degrees.

Toss the sliced peaches with the sugar-cornstarch-spice blend and set aside for a few minutes. Spoon the peaches into the buttered baking dish, along with any juices that may have accumulated.

For the cobbler topping, sift the all-purpose flour, baking powder, and salt into a large mixing bowl. Add the chunks of butter

and shortening and, using 2 round-bladed knives, cut the fat into the flour until it is reduced to small bits. With your fingertips, further reduce the fat to small flakes by dipping down into the mixture and crumbling it. Stir in 2 tablespoons granulated sugar. Pour over the cream-vanilla blend and stir it in with a few quick strokes.

Turn out the dough onto a lightly floured work surface and knead 5 times, then pat it to a thickness of about ¾ inch. Cut biscuits from the dough, using a plain 2½- to 3-inch round biscuit cutter. Place the biscuits on top of the fruit, overlapping them slightly. Sprinkle the remaining 2 teaspoons granulated sugar on top of the biscuits.

Bake the cobbler on a rack in the lower third of the preheated oven for 15 minutes. Reduce the oven temperature to 400 degrees and continue baking for 20 minutes longer, or until the topping is golden brown and the fruit is bubbly.

Serve the cobbler warm or at room temperature.

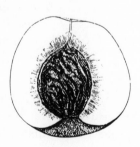

*Cobblers and Crisps*

# Blueberry Crisp

Serve the crisp warm, when the full, rounded flavor of the fruit can best be savored.

[SERVES 6]

**For the blueberries:**

5 cups blueberries, picked over

1/4 cup superfine sugar, or more to taste

2 tablespoons apricot nectar or apple juice

1 tablespoon freshly squeezed lemon juice

1 1/2 teaspoons finely grated lemon peel

**For the butter crumble:**

3/4 cup unsifted all-purpose flour

1/3 cup firmly packed light brown sugar

1/4 cup granulated sugar

1/2 teaspoon freshly grated nutmeg

1/4 teaspoon ground cinnamon

1/4 teaspoon ground ginger

Pinch salt

6 tablespoons (3/4 stick) cold unsalted butter, cut into chunks (or substitute margarine)

Lightly butter an 8-cup ovenproof baking dish that measures about 2 inches deep. Set aside. Preheat the oven to 375 degrees.

Turn the blueberries into a large mixing bowl and toss with the superfine sugar, apricot nectar, lemon juice, and lemon peel. Let stand for 5 minutes, then spoon the blueberries into the baking dish.

For the butter crumble, thoroughly combine the flour, brown sugar, granulated sugar, nutmeg, cinnamon, ginger, and salt in a bowl. Scatter over the cold chunks of butter and, using 2 round-

bladed knives, cut the butter into the flour mixture until it is reduced to small bits. Spoon the crumble evenly over the top of the blueberries.

Bake the crisp on a rack in the lower third of the preheated oven for about 35 to 40 minutes, or until the blueberries are bubbly and the topping is golden and firm.

Transfer the crisp to a cooling rack. Serve warm.

BAKING NOTE: ⅓ cup finely chopped pecans can be added to the crumble topping, if you wish. Stir them in after the butter has been incorporated.

# Cherry-Almond Crisp

Whipped cream, lightly sweetened with confectioners' sugar and flavored with droplets of vanilla extract, is good to serve with this crisp.

[SERVES 6]

**For the cherries:**

4 cups sweet red cherries, stemmed and pitted

2 tablespoons granulated sugar blended with 1½ teaspoons cornstarch

2 tablespoons red current jelly, warmed

2 tablespoons unsalted butter, melted (or substitute margarine)

**For the almond crunch topping:**

¾ cup unsifted all-purpose flour

½ cup firmly packed light brown sugar

¼ teaspoon ground cinnamon

¼ teaspoon freshly grated nutmeg

¼ teaspoon ground allspice

Pinch salt

6 tablespoons (¾ stick) cold unsalted butter, cut into chunks (or substitute margarine)

⅔ cup chopped almonds

Lightly butter an 8-cup ovenproof baking dish that measures about 2 inches deep. Set aside. Preheat the oven to 375 degrees.

Toss the cherries in a mixing bowl with the granulated sugar–cornstarch blend. Let stand 10 minutes. Stir in the warm red currant jelly. Turn the cherry mixture into the prepared baking dish with any of the juices that may have accumulated. Drizzle over the melted butter.

For the topping, combine the flour, light brown sugar, cinnamon, nutmeg, allspice, and salt in a medium-sized mixing bowl.

Add the butter chunks and, using 2 round-bladed knives, cut the butter into the flour mixture until it is reduced to small bits about the size of lentils. Stir in the chopped almonds. Spoon the topping over the layer of cherries.

Bake the crisp on a rack in the lower third of the preheated oven for 35 to 40 minutes, or until the cherries are tender and the topping is golden. (Cover the top of the crisp with a sheet of aluminum foil if the topping begins to darken before the cherries are baked through.)

Transfer the crisp to a cooling rack. Serve warm or at room temperature.

*Cobblers and Crisps*

# Three-Berry Crisp

When you end up with odd assorted lots of fresh berries, toss them in with honey and sprinkle over a buttery nut topping. Once baked, this tempting warm crisp makes a satisfying midsummer dessert. With the exception of strawberries, any combination of berries will do nicely, and they can be sweetened with apple jelly, peach preserves, or plum jam instead of the honey.

[SERVES 6]

**For the berries:**

2 cups blueberries

1 cup red or golden
   raspberries

2 cups blackberries

3 tablespoons honey

**For the walnut-butter topping:**

1 cup chopped walnuts

1/3 cup unsifted all-purpose
   flour

1/3 cup plus 1 tablespoon firmly
   packed light brown sugar

3 tablespoons granulated
   sugar

1/4 teaspoon ground cinnamon

1/4 teaspoon freshly grated
   nutmeg

1/8 teaspoon ground allspice

1/4 teaspoon pure vanilla
   extract

6 tablespoons (3/4 stick) cold
   unsalted butter, cut into
   chunks (or substitute
   margarine)

1 cup crème fraîche (optional)

Lightly butter an 8-cup ovenproof baking dish that measures about 2 inches deep. Set aside. Preheat the oven to 375 degrees.

Pick over the blueberries, raspberries, and blackberries, then toss them in a large bowl with the honey. Spoon the berries into the prepared baking dish.

For the topping, combine the walnuts, flour, light brown sugar,

For the macaroon topping, combine the crumbled macaroons, flour, light brown sugar, granulated sugar, cinnamon, and nutmeg in a mixing bowl. Toss well. Add the chunks of butter and, using 2 round-bladed table knives, cut the butter into the flour mixture until it is reduced to small bits. Spoon the topping over the rhubarb in an even layer.

Bake the crisp on a rack in the lower third of the preheated oven for about 40 to 50 minutes, or until the fruit is tender, the juices are bubbly, and the topping is golden. (If the topping begins to brown too quickly, cover with a sheet of aluminum foil.)

Transfer the crisp to a cooling rack. Serve warm or at room temperature.

NOTE: Stalks of rhubarb generally come to market stripped of leaves; the leaves are poisonous and should not be eaten or used in cooking.

# Cranberry-Pear Crisp

When pears and cranberries abound in the market during the brisk autumn months, it's time to make this dessert. The pear slices turn mellow and silky when baked with the whole cranberries under a blanket of buttery crumbs dotted with pecans.

[SERVES 6]

**For the pears and cranberries:**

*8 firm, ripe pears, stemmed, peeled, cored, sliced, and tossed with 1 tablespoon freshly squeezed lemon juice*
*¼ cup fresh cranberries, picked over*

*¼ cup granulated sugar, or more to taste, blended with ¼ teaspoon ground cinnamon*
*2 tablespoons unsalted butter, melted (or substitute margarine)*

**For the pecan crisp topping:**

*½ cup unsifted all-purpose flour*
*⅓ cup firmly packed light brown sugar*
*3 tablespoons granulated sugar*
*½ teaspoon ground cinnamon*
*½ teaspoon freshly grated nutmeg*

*¼ teaspoon ground ginger*
*Pinch salt*
*7 tablespoons cold unsalted butter, cut into chunks (or substitute margarine)*
*¾ cup chopped pecans*
*1 cup sour cream sweetened with 2 tablespoons pure maple syrup (optional)*

Lightly butter an 8-cup ovenproof baking dish that measures about 2 inches deep. Set aside. Preheat the oven to 375 degrees.

Toss the pears with the cranberries and the sugar-cinnamon blend. Turn into the prepared baking dish. Drizzle the top with the melted butter.

For the pecan crisp topping, combine the flour, light brown sugar, granulated sugar, cinnamon, nutmeg, ginger, and salt in a mixing bowl. Scatter over the chunks of butter and, using 2 round-bladed table knives, cut the butter into the flour mixture until it is reduced to small bits. Stir in the pecans. Crumble the mixture between your fingertips. Cover the top of the pears and cranberries with the pecan mixture.

Bake the crisp on a rack set in the lower third of the preheated oven for 35 to 40 minutes, or until the pears are tender and the topping is golden. (Cover the top with a sheet of aluminum foil if the topping begins to darken before the pears are tender.)

Transfer the crisp to a cooling rack. Serve warm or at room temperature, with the sweetened sour cream, if you like.

# Gingered Pear Crisp

Ripe d'Anjou pears are ideal to use in this crisp.

[SERVES 6]

**For the pears:**

6 large, firm but ripe pears, peeled, halved, cored, and sliced

2 tablespoons honey

1 tablespoon freshly squeezed lemon juice

1 tablespoon chopped ginger preserved in syrup

**For the ginger crisp topping:**

¾ cup finely crushed gingersnaps

¼ cup unsifted all-purpose flour

¼ teaspoon ground ginger

¼ teaspoon ground cinnamon

⅛ teaspoon freshly grated nutmeg

⅓ cup firmly packed light brown sugar

3 tablespoons granulated sugar

5 tablespoons cold unsalted butter, cut into tablespoon chunks (or substitute margarine)

Lightly butter an 8-cup ovenproof baking dish that measures about 2 inches deep. Set aside. Preheat the oven to 375 degrees.

Toss the pears with the honey, lemon juice, and ginger; turn into the prepared baking dish in an even layer.

For the topping, combine the crushed gingersnaps, flour, ginger, cinnamon, nutmeg, light brown sugar, and granulated sugar. Mix well. Scatter the chunks of butter over the top and, using 2 round-bladed table knives, cut the butter into the crumb mixture until it is reduced to small bits. Crumble the mixture between your fingertips. Cover the top of the pears with the topping.

Bake the crisp on a rack in the lower third of the preheated oven for about 35 to 40 minutes, or until the pears are tender.

(Cover the top of the crisp with a sheet of aluminum foil if the topping begins to darken before the pears are tender.)

Transfer the crisp to a cooling rack. Serve warm.

## Pineapple-Macadamia Crisp

I love to serve this pineapple crisp warm, with scoops of pineapple or coconut sherbet. The sherbet builds on the tropical taste of the dessert.

[SERVES 6]

**For the pineapple:**

*4 cups cubed firm but ripe
    pineapple*
*¼ cup apricot nectar*

*1 tablespoon dark rum*
*3 tablespoons superfine sugar*

**For the macadamia topping:**

*½ cup unsifted all-purpose
    flour*
*⅓ cup crushed dry macaroons,
    such as Amaretti*
*¾ teaspoon ground cinnamon*
*¼ teaspoon freshly grated
    nutmeg*
*¼ cup firmly packed light
    brown sugar*

*3 tablespoons granulated
    sugar*
*6 tablespoons (¾ stick) cold
    unsalted butter, cut into
    chunks (or substitute
    margarine)*
*½ cup chopped unsalted
    macadamia nuts*

Lightly butter an 8-cup ovenproof baking dish that measures about 2 inches deep. Set aside. Preheat the oven to 375 degrees.

*(continued)*

*Cobblers and Crisps*

Toss the pineapple cubes with the apricot nectar, rum, and superfine sugar in a mixing bowl. Let stand for 5 minutes, then turn into the prepared baking dish with any juice that may have accumulated.

For the macadamia topping, thoroughly combine the flour, macaroon crumbs, cinnamon, nutmeg, light brown sugar, and granulated sugar in a medium-sized mixing bowl. Add the chunks of butter and, using 2 round-bladed table knives, cut the butter into the flour mixture until it is reduced to small bits. Stir in the macadamia nuts. Spoon the topping over the pineapple in an even layer.

Bake the crisp on a rack in the lower third of the preheated oven for about 40 minutes, or until the topping is golden and set.

Transfer the crisp to a cooling rack. Serve warm or at room temperature.

# Apple Brown Betty

Make the breadcrumbs from fresh, high-quality bread, such as a homemade white bread, egg yolk–enriched challah, or brioche.

[SERVES 4 TO 5]

*1¼ cups fresh breadcrumbs, made from bread trimmed of crusts*
*½ cup granulated sugar blended with 1 teaspoon ground cinnamon and ¼ teaspoon freshly grated nutmeg*

*5 tart cooking apples, peeled, halved, cored, sliced, and tossed with 2 teaspoons freshly squeezed lemon juice*
*3 tablespoons cold unsalted butter, cut into bits (or substitute margarine)*
*⅓ cup apple juice, or apple cider*
*Heavy cream (optional)*

Preheat the oven to 375 degrees. Lightly butter a 6-cup baking dish that is at least 2 inches deep. Set aside.

Toss the breadcrumbs with the sugar and spice blend. Layer half of the apples in the buttered dish and cover with half of the breadcrumb mixture. Dot the top with half of the butter and pour over the apple juice. Layer on the rest of apples, top with the remaining breadcrumbs, and dot with the rest of the butter bits.

Lay a sheet of aluminum foil over the top of the brown betty and bake on a rack in the middle of the preheated oven for 20 minutes. Remove the foil and continue baking for 30 minutes longer, or until the apples are tender and the topping is golden.

Transfer the brown betty to a cooling rack. Serve hot or warm, with heavy cream for pouring over each helping, if you like.

# 5

# Poached, Baked, and Glazed Fruit

White Wine–Poached Pears

Apricot-Poached Pears with Apricot Cream

Vanilla-Scented Apricots with Vanilla Cream

Baked Quince

Rum-Poached Plums with Spiced Custard

Peach Melba

Maple-Baked Apples
Variations: Maple-Baked Apples with Walnuts,
Maple-Baked Apples with Raisins, Maple-Baked Apples with Dried Figs,
Maple-Baked Apples with Dates, Maple-Baked Apples with Dried Apricots

Baked Pears

Ginger-Baked Dried Fruit

Brown Sugar–Grilled Bananas with Rum

Glazed Oranges and Grapefruit Wedges

$\mathrm{A}$ modest sugar syrup—based on water (or juice), sugar, whole spices, and an occasional splash of liqueur or brandy—is capable of transforming plain whole fruit into a memorable dessert. When fruit is simmered in syrup, it emerges spoontender and full of savor. Poached fruit is good on its own, or teamed up with slices of pound cake or flavored butter cake. The cooked fruit looks pretty layered in a clear glass cylinder or bowl, with its syrup partially submerging the fruit, giving it a light, crystalline quality.

Plums, apricots, and pears fare exceedingly well in the poaching process: A syrup brings out all the subtle, rounded flavors of the fruit and the slow, gentle cooking process keeps the curvy shapes intact.

Summer fruit, in contrast to the substantial fruit of autumn and winter, needs only a quick simmering in liquid to be perfectly cooked. In addition to a sauce, a plate of cookies or sliced sponge cake would be a welcome accompaniment. For gift-giving, consider putting up jars of plums or apricots; to do so, just double the amount of poaching liquid so that there will be plenty of syrup to cover the fruit once it is transferred to a sturdy container. The preserved fruit, drained and sliced or chopped, is terrific to have on hand to add to mousse mixtures, ice cream bases, dessert sauces, or custard puddings.

Glazed fruit—slices of lightly sweetened fruit run under a hot broiler—makes a fast and tasty dessert. In this chapter, sliced bananas and slices of winter citrus, notably grapefruit and orange sections, are sugared and grilled. And remember that ripe peaches, apricots, or nectarines, when in season, can be peeled, sliced, and arranged overlapping in a gratin dish, topped with brown sugar, drizzled with rum or bourbon, and grilled. Crème fraîche, touched with liquid brown sugar or maple syrup and freshly grated nutmeg, is delicious dolloped over helpings of grilled bananas or the sliced summer fruit.

## White Wine–Poached Pears

This white wine syrup accentuates the mellow flavor of fresh pears. The pears can be poached whole, as I have described below, or they can be peeled, halved, cored, and baked in the syrup in a moderately low oven until just tender.

Pass a basket of plain butter cookies with the pears, if you wish.

[SERVES 6]

¾ cup granulated sugar          Half a lemon
1⅓ cups water                   6 firm, ripe pears, such as
1 cup dry white wine                Bosc or d'Anjou
1 vanilla bean

Place the granulated sugar, water, white wine, and vanilla bean in a heavy nonreactive 6-quart casserole. Cover, place over low

*Fruit Desserts*

heat, and cook until the sugar has dissolved completely. Uncover, raise the heat to high, and bring to the boil; boil for 2 minutes.

While the syrup is cooking, fill a large bowl with cold water and squeeze in the juice from the half lemon. Peel the pears, leaving the stems intact, and slip them into the bowl of acidulated water as they are peeled.

Remove the pears from the water and add to the syrup. Simmer the pears in the syrup, covered, until they are tender, about 25 minutes (more or less according to the ripeness of the fruit), basting the pears every 5 minutes.

When the pears are tender, carefully remove the casserole from the heat and let stand for 15 minutes. Transfer the pears to a heatproof dish or bowl. (I use a pair of soft rubber spatulas to dip out the pears.) Return the casserole to the heat and boil the syrup until it is thickened, about 5 minutes. Pour the syrup over the pears and sink the vanilla bean into the syrup as well. (The pears may be prepared up to 3 days in advance of serving; transfer the cooled pears and syrup to a container, cover, and refrigerate.)

Serve the pears warm, at room temperature, or chilled, with some of the syrup spooned over.

# Apricot-Poached Pears
## with Apricot Cream

A basket of nut crescents or crisp spice wafers is a nice accompaniment to the pears.

[SERVES 6]

*Half a lemon*
*6 firm, ripe pears, such as*
*  Bosc or d'Anjou*
*1½ cups water*
*1 cup apricot nectar*
*½ cup apricot schnapps*

*½ cup granulated sugar*
*1 cinnamon stick*
*6 whole allspice berries*
*6 whole cloves*
*6 dried apricot halves*

**For the apricot cream:**

*⅔ cup sour cream*
*3 tablespoons milk*

*The puréed apricots (see*
*  below)*

Fill a large bowl with cold water and squeeze in the juice from the half lemon. Peel the pears, leaving the stems intact, and slip them into the bowl of acidulated water as they are peeled.

Place the 1½ cups water, apricot nectar, schnapps, sugar, cinnamon stick, allspice berries, whole cloves, and dried apricot halves in a heavy nonreactive 6-quart casserole. Cover, set over low heat, and cook until every grain of sugar has dissolved. Uncover, bring to the boil, and boil for 3 minutes. Drain the pears and put them in the syrup solution. Adjust the heat so that the syrup simmers gently, cover, and cook the pears for about 25 minutes (cooking time will depend on the degree of ripeness of the fruit), basting them frequently. (The best way to baste fruit as it poaches, I've learned over the years, is to use a rubber bulb baster—the same piece of equipment used to baste the Thanksgiving turkey. A bulb

baster efficiently draws up the poaching liquid and squirts it over the fruit without nicking, bruising, or denting the flesh.)

Carefully remove the cooked pears to a heatproof bowl. Boil the syrup (with the apricots) for 4 or 5 minutes, or until lightly condensed. Remove the casserole from the heat. Discard the spices. Place the apricots and ¼ cup of the poaching liquid in the bowl of a food processor fitted with the steel blade or in the container of a blender; purée the apricots and scrape the mixture into a bowl. Pour the remaining syrup over the pears. (The pears and apricot purée may be made up to 3 days in advance of serving. Transfer the cooled pears and syrup to a storage container, cover, and refrigerate; transfer the puréed apricots to a storage container, cover, and refrigerate.)

If you have made the pears in advance, remove them from the refrigerator about 15 minutes before serving.

For the apricot cream, mix the sour cream, milk, and puréed apricot mixture in a bowl.

Place each poached pear in a deep dessert plate, pour over a little of the syrup, and spoon a bit of the apricot cream to one side of the pear. Serve immediately.

*Poached, Baked, and Glazed Fruit*

# Vanilla-Scented Apricots
## with Vanilla Cream

Poaching apricots in a syrup enhanced with a split vanilla bean intensifies the subtle perfumelike qualities of the fruit.

[SERVES 6]

**For the syrup:**

*½ cup granulated sugar*
*Pinch salt*
*1¾ cups water*

*¼ cup apricot schnapps*
*1 vanilla bean*

*18 whole fresh apricots*

**For the vanilla cream:**

*½ cup heavy cream*
*½ cup sour cream*
*3 tablespoons poaching syrup*

*1 teaspoon pure vanilla*
*extract*

For the syrup, place the granulated sugar, salt, water, apricot schnapps, and vanilla bean in a heavy 2-quart casserole. Cover, set over low heat, and cook until the sugar has dissolved completely. Uncover, raise the heat to high, bring to the boil, and boil for 2 minutes. Add the whole apricots, reduce the heat to low, and simmer for 5 minutes, or until the fruit is tender, spooning some of the cooking liquid over the apricots as they cook.

With a slotted spoon, remove the apricots to a shallow bowl. Bring the syrup to a boil and boil until lightly thickened and glossy, about 2 minutes. Strain the syrup into a bowl and cool. When the apricots are cool enough to handle, halve them and remove the pits. Pour the cooled syrup over them. (The apricots may be prepared up to 1 week in advance; cover tightly and refrigerate.)

*Fruit Desserts*

For the vanilla cream, blend the heavy cream, sour cream, syrup, and vanilla extract, in a small bowl.

Spoon the apricots onto deep dessert plates. Spoon a bit of the vanilla cream over each helping of fruit and serve.

## Baked Quince

Serve the wedges of oven-baked quince with heavy cream or custard sauce.

[SERVES 4]

4 quince, peeled, halved,
   cored, and cut into thick
   wedges
½ cup firmly packed light
   brown sugar
1 teaspoon finely grated lemon
   peel

2 cups apple juice
2 tablespoons unsalted butter,
   cut into bits (or substitute
   margarine)

Preheat the oven to 325 degrees.

Place half of the quince wedges in a heavy 6-cup nonreactive ovenproof casserole (preferably enameled cast iron). Sprinkle over half of the brown sugar and all the lemon peel. Top with the remaining quince and sprinkle with the balance of the brown sugar. Pour the apple juice over all and dot the top with the butter bits. Cover the casserole.

Bake the quince on a rack in the middle of the preheated oven for about 1 hour 15 minutes, or until the fruit is fork-tender.

Transfer the baked quince to a cooling rack and uncover the casserole. Serve warm or at room temperature.

*Poached, Baked, and Glazed Fruit*

# Rum-Poached Plums
# with Spiced Custard

This is a dessert that glamorizes summer's juicy plums. If you love plums as much as I do, you'll put up a jar of them in this syrup to have on hand.

[ SERVES 4 ]

*16 small red plums*

**For the rum syrup:**

*1½ cups water*
*½ cup dark rum*
*⅓ cup granulated sugar*

*1 cinnamon stick*
*6 whole allspice berries*
*1 small vanilla bean*

**For the spiced custard:**

*½ cup milk*
*½ cup light cream*
*½ cup heavy cream*
*2 tablespoons superfine sugar blended with 1½ teaspoons arrowroot, ¼ teaspoon ground cinnamon, ⅛ teaspoon freshly grated nutmeg, and ⅛ teaspoon ground ginger*

*4 extra-large egg yolks, at room temperature*
*¾ teaspoon pure vanilla extract*
*Superfine sugar for dusting*

Prick the plums with the tip of a skewer. Set aside.

Place the water, rum, sugar, cinnamon stick, allspice berries, and vanilla bean in a heavy nonreactive 4-quart casserole. Cover, place over low heat, and cook until the sugar dissolves completely. Uncover, raise the heat to high, and bring to the boil; boil for

2 minutes. Reduce the heat to low, add the plums, and simmer for 3 minutes, or until the plums are just tender, spooning the syrup over and about the plums as they cook.

With a slotted spoon, remove the plums from the syrup to a bowl. Bring the syrup to a boil over high heat and boil until slightly reduced, about 2 or 3 minutes. Remove from the heat and cool completely; remove and discard the allspice berries.

When the plums are cool enough to handle, carefully slip off the skins. Place the plums in a jar or serving bowl and pour over the syrup (including the cinnamon stick and vanilla bean—they will continue to add flavor to the fruit). Refrigerate the plums, tightly covered, for up to 1 month.

For the spiced custard, scald the milk, light cream, and heavy cream in a small saucepan; set aside. Place the sugar blend and the egg yolks in a small heavy saucepan and beat for 2 minutes. Strain the hot scalded liquid over the yolk mixture in a thin stream, blending well. Place the saucepan over low heat and cook slowly, stirring, until the mixture thickens, coats the back of a wooden spoon, and registers 175 degrees on a candy thermometer. Remove from the heat and stir in the vanilla extract. Strain the custard into a pitcher or small bowl. Dust the top with a little superfine sugar to prevent a skin from forming, or place a sheet of plastic wrap directly over the top. (The custard can be made up to 2 days in advance. Refrigerate the cooled custard in an airtight container.)

For each serving, spoon 4 plums and a little of the rum syrup on each deep dessert plate. Add a pouring of the spiced custard and serve immediately.

*Poached, Baked, and Glazed Fruit*

# Peach Melba

Make this classic summertime dessert with ripe white peaches or juicy freestone peaches.

[SERVES 6]

**For the peaches:**

*2¾ cups water*
*¾ cup granulated sugar*

*3 strips lemon peel*
*6 firm, ripe peaches, peeled*

**For the raspberry sauce:**

*2 cups ripe, red raspberries,*
*   picked over*
*¼ cup red currant jelly*

*1 teaspoon freshly squeezed*
*   lemon juice*
*1 tablespoon water*

*6 scoops vanilla ice cream,*
*   homemade or store-bought*

For the peaches, place the water, sugar, and lemon peel in a medium-sized nonreactive casserole. Cover, place over low heat, and cook until every grain of sugar has dissolved. Uncover, bring to the boil, and boil 3 minutes. Slip in the whole peaches and poach them until tender, about 3 to 5 minutes. Carefully remove the peaches to a shallow bowl and spoon about 1 cup of the poaching liquid over them. Cool the peaches to room temperature, then cover and refrigerate. (The peaches may be poached and refrigerated up to 3 days in advance.)

For the raspberry sauce, combine the raspberries, red currant jelly, lemon juice, and water in a medium-sized nonreactive saucepan. Place over moderate heat and cook, stirring occasionally, until the raspberries are completely softened and slightly thickened.

Remove from the heat. Purée the raspberry mixture through a food mill fitted with the fine disk. Cool the sauce completely and refrigerate in a covered container. (The raspberry sauce may be prepared up to 2 weeks in advance.)

For each serving, carefully halve the peaches and remove the pits. Place a scoop of ice cream in each shallow bowl, set 2 peach halves to one side, and spoon a pool of raspberry sauce (about 3 tablespoons) around the ice cream and peaches. Serve immediately.

*Poached, Baked, and Glazed Fruit*

# Maple-Baked Apples

$\mathbb{F}$irm, creamy-textured cooking apples take well to stuffing with sugar and spices and baking in a pool of apple cider and maple syrup. To vary the apple filling, you can add dark or golden raisins, dried currants, dried fruit, or lightly toasted walnuts to the sugar blend. These homestyle apples are delightful served hot or warm, with the syrupy pan juices spooned over. If you wish, serve with vanilla ice cream, custard sauce, or heavy cream.

[SERVES 8]

8 firm cooking apples, such as
　Stayman, winesap, or Rome
　Beauty
⅓ cup firmly packed light
　brown sugar
¾ teaspoon ground cinnamon
½ teaspoon freshly grated
　nutmeg

Pinch ground allspice
Pinch ground cloves
1½ cups fresh apple cider,
　preferably unfiltered (or
　more as needed), or apple
　juice
2 tablespoons pure maple
　syrup

Lightly butter a 9 × 12-inch nonreactive baking dish. Set aside. Preheat the oven to 350 degrees.

Cut off thin slices from the bottom of each apple if they do not sit upright; core each apple, cutting out a deep cavity from the top. The cavity should be large enough to hold a spoonful of the stuffing mixture.

Mix the light brown sugar, cinnamon, nutmeg, allspice, and cloves in small bowl. Fill the core of each apple with some of the sugar and spice mixture, dividing it evenly. Scatter any extra filling on the bottom of the baking dish.

Arrange the apples in the baking pan and pour the apple cider and maple syrup around them. Bake the apples in the preheated oven for about 40 minutes, or until tender throughout, basting

them occasionally with the cider. (Test the apples for tenderness with a toothpick or the tip of a skewer; overbaked apples tend to collapse.) Add more apple cider to the bottom of the baking pan as the apples bake, if the liquid cooks down too low.

Cool the apples in the pan for 5 minutes, then carefully remove them with a slotted spoon. (If the pan juices have not condensed lightly, pour into a saucepan and reduce over high heat for a minute or two.) Serve the apples hot or warm, with some of the pan juices poured over them.

### Variations

For *Maple-Baked Apples with Walnuts*, add ¼ cup lightly toasted chopped walnuts to the sugar and spice blend.

For *Maple-Baked Apples with Raisins*, add ¼ cup (about 1½ ounces) seedless golden raisins to the sugar and spice blend.

For *Maple-Baked Apples with Dried Figs*, stem and coarsely chop 4 (about 3 ounces) moist, dried figs. Add the figs to the sugar and spice blend.

For *Maple-Baked Apples with Dates*, coarsely chop 5 (about 1½ ounces) pitted dried or fresh dates. Add the dates to the sugar and spice blend.

For *Maple-Baked Apples with Dried Apricots*, coarsely chop 5 (about 1 ounce) dried apricot halves. Add the apricots to the sugar and spice blend.

# Baked Pears

Serve the pears with a plate of crisp gingersnaps or soft spice cookies.

2½ *cups white grape juice*
2 *tablespoons granulated*
  *sugar*
5 *strips lemon peel*
4 *whole cloves*

1 *cinnamon stick*
6 *firm, ripe pears, such as*
  *d'Anjou or Bosc, peeled,*
  *stemmed, halved, and*
  *cored*

Preheat the oven to 350 degrees.

Place the grape juice, sugar, lemon peel, cloves, and cinnamon stick in a large oval nonreactive casserole (preferably enameled cast iron). Cover, place over low heat, and cook until the grains of sugar have dissolved completely. Uncover, bring to the boil, and boil for 1 minute. Remove from the heat, slip in the pears, rounded sides up, and cover tightly.

Bake the pears on a rack in the middle of the preheated oven for 25 to 30 minutes, or until just tender, basting them with the grape juice from time to time.

Transfer the pears to a cooling rack, uncover, and let stand for 10 minutes, basting them once or twice with the cooking liquid. Discard the lemon peel and cloves. Serve warm, at room temperature, or chilled. (The pears may be made up to 1 week in advance. Carefully lift them into a storage container. Pour over the cooking liquid, add the cinnamon stick, cover, and refrigerate.)

# Ginger-Baked Dried Fruit

Lightly sweetened with brown sugar and spiced with sliced preserved ginger, this compote of dried fruit makes a soothing cold-weather dessert.

[SERVES 5 TO 6]

3 cups (about 1¼ pounds) mixed moist dried fruit (choose from dried apricots, pears, peaches, figs, apples, prunes, dates, raisins, and currants)

¼ cup firmly packed light brown sugar

1 tablespoon sliced ginger preserved in syrup

1 tablespoon syrup from preserved ginger

3 cups apple juice, or apple cider

1 cinnamon stick

Heavy cream or sour cream (optional)

Preheat the oven to 350 degrees.

Layer the fruit (except for dates, raisins, or currants) with the brown sugar and ginger in a 4-quart nonreactive casserole. Pour over the apple juice and bury the cinnamon stick in the fruit.

Cover the casserole and bake the fruit on a rack in the middle of the preheated oven for 35 minutes, or until the fruit is tender, stirring the fruit a few times while it bakes. Add dates, raisins, or currants to the casserole for the final 6 to 8 minutes of cooking time.

Remove the casserole from the oven, set the lid ajar, and let cool slightly. Discard the cinnamon stick, if you like, or leave it in for extra flavor. (The fruit may be served now or transferred to a storage container, covered, and refrigerated for up to 1 month.)

Serve the fruit hot, warm, at room temperature, or chilled, in small bowls with heavy cream or sour cream, if you wish.

*Poached, Baked, and Glazed Fruit*

# Brown Sugar-Grilled
## Bananas with Rum

These bananas are tasty as is—or served with dollops of sour cream.

¼ cup water
¼ cup dark rum
2 tablespoons firmly packed
   light brown sugar
7 tablespoons unsalted butter
   (or substitute margarine)

6 firm, ripe bananas
5 tablespoons firmly packed
   light brown sugar blended
   with ½ teaspoon ground
   cinnamon and ¼ teaspoon
   freshly grated nutmeg

Lightly grease a jelly roll pan. Set aside. Preheat the broiler to high.

Combine the water, rum, 2 tablespoons brown sugar, and 2 tablespoons of the butter in a small saucepan. Cover, set over moderately low heat, and cook until the sugar dissolves completely. Uncover, bring to the boil, boil 1 minute, and set aside.

Peel the bananas, slice in half lengthwise, and arrange on the baking sheet. Dot the tops of the bananas with the remaining 5 tablespoons butter, cubed. Crumble over the light brown sugar-spice blend.

Grill the bananas under the broiler until golden, watching carefully, about 2 or 3 minutes.

Transfer the bananas to warm plates, 2 halves to a serving, and drizzle a bit of the rum syrup over each serving.

# Glazed Orange and Grapefruit Wedges

You could top the glazed citrus with thin threads of orange peel, simmered in sugar syrup until translucent.

[SERVES 6]

*1/3 cup water*
*3 tablespoons orange liqueur*
*1 1/2 tablespoons granulated sugar*
*4 large pink grapefruit, peeled and cut into sections, at room temperature*

*4 large seedless (navel) oranges, peeled and cut into sections, at room temperature*
*3 tablespoons maple sugar, or 2 tablespoons firmly packed light brown sugar*

Preheat the broiler to high.

For the syrup, place the water, orange liqueur, and granulated sugar in a small nonreactive saucepan. Cover, set over low heat, and cook until the sugar dissolves completely. Uncover, bring to the boil, simmer 1 minute, and set aside.

Arrange the grapefruit and orange sections, overlapping slightly, in a nonreactive 5- or 6-cup ovenproof baking dish. Spoon over the syrup. Sprinkle the top of the fruit with the maple or light brown sugar.

Grill the fruit 3 inches from the heat source until the patches of sugar on top turn golden. Watch carefully to prevent scorching.

Serve the fruit immediately.

# 6

# Ice Creams and Sherbets, Floats and Sodas

### Peach Ice Cream
*Variations: Blueberry Ice Cream, Huckleberry Ice Cream, Nectarine Ice Cream, Fig Ice Cream, Strawberry Ice Cream, Prune-Armagnac Ice Cream*

### Apple Ice Cream
*Variation: Cherry-Vanilla Ice Cream*

### Orange Ice
*Variations: Pineapple Ice, Lemon Ice, Apple Ice, Peach Ice*

### Creamy Pineapple Sherbet
*Variation: Creamy Lime Sherbet*

### Peach Sodas

### Raspberry Cream Sodas

### Lemon Floats

$O$ftentimes, the flavor of fresh fruit—mellow, tangy, or sweet-tart—is enhanced by the addition of cream, or a creamy element. A simple fruit compote, for example, becomes a special dessert when served with a ladle of custard sauce. A fruit purée turns into a luxurious fool when you spoon it through lightly whipped cream. But the combination of fruit and cream is perhaps most seductive in churned desserts and soda fountain treats: Who would turn down a bowl of ice cream speckled with sweet huckleberries or summer's ripe strawberries? Or what about a tall float made up of lemon sherbet and freshly squeezed lemonade?

When shopping at the farmers' market, remember that overripe whole fruit is ideal for puréeing and using in ice cream, as is slightly blemished fruit that has been carefully trimmed. Berries, however, should be firm, plump, and free of mold.

Serve any of the cooling and refreshing desserts in this chapter with a plate of crispy cookies: Thin and crackly, flecked with nuts or flavored with spices, these are the perfect foil to what you dip out of the ice cream freezer.

*Ice Creams and Sherbets, Floats and Sodas*

# Peach Ice Cream

The custard base for this ice cream can be used with a range of fruit and berries. To flavor ice cream, summer's ripe fruit needs only to be puréed in a blender or food processor before combining with the ice cream base.

This ice cream and the variations that follow will hold beautifully in the freezer for at least 1 week. About 15 to 20 minutes before serving, transfer the ice cream to the refrigerator to soften a bit.

[SERVES 4 TO 6]

4 extra-large egg yolks, at
   room temperature
1/2 cup granulated sugar
1 1/4 cups milk, at room
   temperature
3/4 cup heavy cream, at room
   temperature

Pinch salt
1 1/2 cups cold light cream
1/2 cup cold heavy cream
4 fragrant, ripe peaches,
   peeled, halved, pitted, and
   cut into chunks

Beat the egg yolks and granulated sugar until thick in a heavy medium-sized saucepan. Blend in the milk, 3/4 cup heavy cream, and salt. Place over low heat and cook, stirring, until the mixture thickens lightly, coats the back of a wooden spoon, and registers 175 degrees on a candy thermometer. Strain the mixture into a bowl and cool completely. Stir in the light cream and 1/2 cup heavy cream. Cover and refrigerate until cold, about 8 hours. (The custard base may be prepared up to 3 days in advance.)

Purée the peaches in the container of a blender or in the bowl of the food processor fitted with the steel blade. Stir the peach purée into the chilled custard base. Churn the mixture in an ice cream maker according to the manufacturer's directions.

Spoon the ice cream into a sturdy storage container, cover, and place in the freezer to cure for at least 2 hours before serving.

*Fruit Desserts*

*Variations*

For *Blueberry Ice Cream*, substitute for the peaches 1¼ cups blueberries, picked over.

For *Huckleberry Ice Cream*, substitute for the peaches 1½ cups huckleberries, picked over.

For *Nectarine Ice Cream*, substitute for the peaches 4 ripe nectarines, peeled, halved, pitted, and cut into chunks.

For *Fig Ice Cream*, simmer 1 cup (8 ounces) stemmed dried figs in 1½ cups unsweetened apple juice to cover for 30 to 35 minutes, or until very tender. Purée the figs along with ⅓ cup of the cooking liquid, and use in place of the peach purée.

For *Strawberry Ice Cream*, substitute for the peaches 1½ cups strawberries, hulled.

For *Prune-Armagnac Ice Cream*, simmer 1 cup (about 6 ounces) dried pitted prunes in 1 cup apple juice for 20 minutes, or until very tender. Purée the prunes along with ¼ cup of the cooking liquid. Place ¼ cup Armagnac in a saucepan, bring to a boil, and simmer until reduced to about 1½ tablespoons. Stir the Armagnac into the puréed prunes and use in place of the peach purée.

# Apple Ice Cream

Serve scoops of this ice cream with hot caramel or butter-scotch sauce, with warm slabs of apple pie, apple cobbler, or apple crisp, or with slices of oatmeal cake.

[SERVES 5 TO 6]

*3 tart cooking apples, peeled, cored, and sliced*

*¼ cup granulated sugar blended with 2 teaspoons ground cinnamon, ½ teaspoon freshly grated nutmeg, and ⅛ teaspoon ground cloves*

*¼ cup apple cider*

*1 cup light cream, at room temperature*

*1 cup milk, at room temperature*

*½ cup granulated sugar*

*Pinch salt*

*1 tablespoon pure vanilla extract*

*2 cups cold heavy cream*

For the apple mixture, place the apple slices, granulated sugar-spice blend, and apple cider in a medium-sized nonreactive sauce-pan. Set over moderately low heat and cook until the sugar dissolves completely, stirring occasionally. Cook the apples for 10 to 12 minutes longer, or until they have softened completely and have turned to mush. Uncover the saucepan and cook for 1 min-ute. Thoroughly crush the apples with the back of a spoon or a potato masher and set aside. (The apple mixture can be made up to 3 weeks in advance; refrigerate in an airtight container.)

Place the light cream, milk, ½ cup granulated sugar, and salt in a saucepan, set over low heat, and cook until the sugar dissolves. Remove from the heat and cool completely. Stir in the vanilla extract and heavy cream. Refrigerate until cold, about 6 to 8 hours.

Stir the chilled apple mixture into the heavy cream mixture and churn in an ice cream maker according to the directions supplied by the manufacturer.

Spoon the ice cream into a sturdy storage container, cover, and place in the freezer to cure for at least 2 hours before serving.

*Variation*

For *Cherry-Vanilla Ice Cream*, omit the apples, sugar-spice blend, and apple cider. Simmer 1½ cups red cherries, stemmed and pitted, in 2 cups unsweetened apple juice until very tender, about 20 minutes. Cool completely. Remove the cherries from the poaching liquid with a slotted spoon and chop coarsely. Add half a vanilla bean, split down the center, to the light cream, milk, and sugar mixture as it warms; when cool enough to handle, scrape the vanilla bean seeds into the liquid.

# Orange Ice

Water ices, made up of fruit juice, sugar, and water, taste best when churned in an ice cream maker and eaten when slushy.

[SERVES 5]

1³/4 cups water
1 cup granulated sugar
1¹/4 cups freshly squeezed
   orange juice

1¹/4 teaspoons finely grated
   orange peel

Place the water and sugar in a large nonreactive saucepan. Cover, set over low heat, and cook until every grain of sugar has dissolved. Uncover the saucepan, raise the heat to high, and bring the liquid to a boil. Boil for 5 minutes. Stir in the orange juice and simmer for 2 minutes. Remove from the heat and stir in the orange peel. Cool completely. Transfer the ice base to a storage container, cover, and refrigerate until cold. (The base may be made ahead up to 2 weeks in advance.)

Churn the chilled mixture in an ice cream maker according to the directions supplied by the manufacturer. Serve the ice immediately (or store it in the freezer for up to 1 hour, stirring vigorously before serving).

## Variations

For *Pineapple Ice*, substitute for the orange juice 2 cups unsweetened pineapple juice, reduce the amount of water to 1¹/4 cups, reduce the sugar to ³/4 cup, and substitute 1¹/4 teaspoons lemon peel for the orange peel.

For *Lemon Ice*, substitute for the orange juice ¾ cup freshly squeezed lemon juice, and 1¼ teaspoons lemon peel for the orange peel.

For *Apple Ice*, substitute for the orange juice 2 cups apple juice, reduce the amount of water to 1¼ cups, and reduce the sugar to ¾ cup. Omit the orange peel.

For *Peach Ice*, substitute for the orange juice 1½ cups peach nectar and ½ cup peach purée (to make peach purée, see recipe for Frozen Peach Mousse on page 98), reduce the amount of water to 1¼ cups, and reduce the sugar to ¾ cup. Substitute 1¼ teaspoons lemon peel for the orange peel.

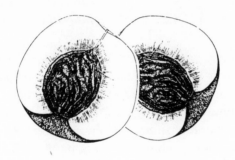

# Creamy Pineapple Sherbet

This sherbet is easily made with dairy and pantry staples—canned unsweetened pineapple juice, a sugar syrup, milk, and heavy cream. Scoops of sherbet, served in pretty glass flutes, are delicious paired with rolled sugar cookies or gaufrettes.

My mother made a sweet and tart creamy lime sherbet (see variation that follows) and this recipe is modeled after hers.

[SERVES 4]

*3/4 cup water*
*3/4 cup granulated sugar*
*1 1/2 tablespoons light corn syrup*
*1 1/4 cups cold milk*

*1/3 cup cold heavy cream*
*1 teaspoon finely grated lemon peel*
*1 cup chilled unsweetened pineapple juice*

Place the water, sugar, and corn syrup in a small saucepan, cover, and set over low heat; cook slowly until the sugar dissolves completely. Uncover the pan, raise the heat to high, and bring to a boil; boil 1 minute. Remove from the heat and cool completely. Pour into a storage container, cover, and refrigerate until well chilled, about 6 hours. (The syrup may be made up to 1 week in advance.)

Blend together the chilled sugar syrup, milk, heavy cream, lemon peel, and pineapple juice in a bowl. Churn the mixture in an ice cream maker according to the directions supplied by the manufacturer. Turn the sherbet into a storage container and let cure in the freezer for 1 to 2 hours before serving.

### Variation

To make *Creamy Lime Sherbet*, substitute 3/4 cup freshly squeezed lime juice for the pineapple juice and 2 teaspoons freshly grated

lime peel for the lemon peel. Add 2 tablespoons defrosted limeade concentrate to the chilled sugar syrup, milk, heavy cream, lime peel, and lime juice. Two tablespoons chopped fresh spearmint or peppermint may be added to the sherbet mixture about 5 minutes before it is finished churning.

# Peach Sodas

Pass a basket of gingersnaps, lemon wafers, or macadamia nut crisps to nibble with the sodas.

[SERVES 4]

*1 1/3 cups peeled, seeded, and
    diced ripe peaches*

**For each soda:**

*1/4 cup cold milk
1/3 cup cold seltzer
3 tablespoons peach purée (see
    below)*

*Vanilla ice cream (see
    Raspberry Cream Sodas on
    page 154 for recipe)*

Place the peach chunks in the bowl of a food processor fitted with the steel blade, or in the container of a blender, and purée.

To assemble each soda, pour the milk and seltzer into a large glass. Stir in 3 tablespoons of the peach purée. Add 2 scoops of ice cream, stir gently, and serve.

NOTE: A few thinly sliced peaches may be added to each soda along with the ice cream, if you wish.

*Ice Creams and Sherbets, Floats and Sodas*

# Raspberry Cream Sodas

Homemade vanilla ice cream, fresh raspberry syrup, and a spritz of seltzer make up this tantalizing beverage. Cooling and sweet, the soda is a liquid dessert that can cap off any light supper during the sun-stroked days of summer. If you have a good supply of fresh raspberries on hand, embellish each soda with a few tablespoons of them, spooning the berries into the glass after you've added the ice cream. Then add a long spoon to each glass for eating the ice cream and berries together.

[SERVES 6]

**For the vanilla ice cream:**

1 cup milk
1¼ cups light cream
3 extra-large egg yolks, at room temperature
½ cup plus 2 tablespoons granulated sugar
Pinch salt

Seed scrapings from the inside of half a vanilla bean
1 tablespoon pure vanilla extract
1½ cups cold milk
¾ cup cold heavy cream

**For the raspberry syrup:**

2½ cups red, ripe raspberries
¾ cup granulated sugar

1 teaspoon freshly squeezed lemon juice
½ cup water

**For each soda:**

⅓ cup cold milk
⅓ cup cold seltzer
2 scoops vanilla ice cream

2 tablespoons fresh raspberry syrup
2 tablespoons red, ripe raspberries (optional)

For the vanilla ice cream, whisk together the milk, ¾ cup light cream, egg yolks, granulated sugar, salt, and vanilla bean scrapings in a heavy saucepan. Set over low heat and cook, stirring all the while, until the mixture thickens, coats the back of a wooden spoon, and registers 175 degrees on a candy thermometer. Remove from the heat and stir in the vanilla extract. Strain into a bowl. Stir in the cold milk, heavy cream, and remaining ½ cup light cream. Turn into a storage container, cover, and refrigerate until very cold, about 6 to 8 hours. (The ice cream mixture may be made up to 1 week in advance.)

Churn the mixture in an ice cream maker according to the directions supplied by the manufacturer. Turn the ice cream into a storage container, cover, and let cure in the freezer for 1 to 2 hours before using.

For the raspberry syrup, place the raspberries, sugar, lemon juice, and water in a 2-quart nonreactive casserole. Cover, place over moderately low heat, and cook until the sugar dissolves completely and the raspberries are quite soft; stir the contents of the casserole from time to time. Strain the mixture through a stainless-steel sieve. Cool the syrup completely, then refrigerate in a covered container.

To assemble each soda, pour the milk and seltzer into a large glass. Add 2 scoops of vanilla ice cream and pour on 2 tablespoons of the raspberry syrup. Stir gently. Sprinkle the raspberries on the top and serve with a straw and a tall spoon.

NOTE: These may be made with a good-quality store-bought vanilla ice cream.

# Lemon Floats

Served in a tall ribbed glass, this float will bring back memories of soda shop days—when you would slide onto a stool and order your favorite sweet. This is a lemon lover's delight: scoops of home-churned sherbet melting into cold, fresh lemonade and club soda.

[SERVES 5]

**For the lemon sherbet:**

3/4 cup water
3/4 cup granulated sugar
2 teaspoons finely grated lemon peel
1 1/3 cups milk

1/4 cup heavy cream
1/2 cup plus 2 tablespoons cold freshly squeezed lemon juice (2 to 3 lemons)

**For the lemonade:**

1/2 cup water
3/4 cup granulated sugar

About 3 cups cold water
3/4 cup freshly squeezed lemon juice (about 4 lemons)

1 1/4 cups cold seltzer

For the lemon sherbet, place the sugar and water in a small nonreactive saucepan, cover, set over low heat, and cook until the sugar has dissolved completely. Uncover, raise the heat to moderately high, and bring the sugar-water to a boil; boil 2 minutes. Cool completely.

Combine the sugar syrup, lemon peel, milk, and heavy cream, in a bowl. Refrigerate for 1 hour. Stir in the lemon juice. Churn the mixture in an ice cream maker according to the directions supplied by the manufacturer. Turn the sherbet into a storage

container, cover, and freeze until needed. (The sherbet may be made up to 1 week in advance.)

For the lemonade, place the ½ cup water and the sugar in a small nonreactive saucepan, cover, set over low heat, and cook until the sugar has dissolved completely. Uncover, raise the heat to moderately high, and bring the sugar-water to a boil. Boil for 3 minutes. Cool completely. Stir in the lemon juice and cold water, adding a little more cold water if the lemonade seems too strong. Chill the lemonade until needed.

To make the floats, place scoops of sherbet in tall glasses, pour in lemonade until each glass is about half full, then add ¼ cup seltzer to each glass. Stir gently and serve.

*Ice Creams and Sherbets, Floats and Sodas*

# 7

# Gifts of
# Preserved Fruit

*Fruit butters*

*Fruit compotes*

Nowadays, I put up jars of fruit butter and compotes, in addition to savory fruit chutneys and sauces, in small batches, and store these in the refrigerator to use in everyday cooking and dessert-making. As each season progresses, the largess gets used in all kinds of preparations; then it's time to start over again a few months later with a new supply of seasonal fruit. Small quantities of preserved fruit are far less time-consuming to prepare and, I think, taste better, too. But most of all, a jar of preserved fruit makes a lovely bread-and-butter hostess gift.

Two of my very favorite projects are the making of fruit butters and fruit compotes—either one is lovely to have on hand for enhancing many kinds of desserts. Spoon the preserved mixture into one large container, label, refrigerate, and parcel out portions into decorative jars just before gift-giving. Or pack up the goods in individual jars, seal, label, and leave in the refrigerator until needed.

*Gifts of Preserved Fruit*

# Fruit Butters

Fruit butter, a spread that tastes like the essence of the fruit from which it is made, is mellow and velvety. You can spread fruit butter on the bottom of a baked tart shell before adding a fresh berry filling, fold half a cup of the butter into an ice cream base right before it is churned, or whisk a few tablespoons into a custard mixture or fruit sauce to deepen the flavor. Apples, pears, nectarines, peaches (white and yellow), plums, or apricots are all excellent sources for fruit butters.

For apple or pear butter, peel and core 3½ pounds of fruit. Cut into chunks and place in a large nonreactive casserole. Pour over 1¼ cups of water, cover, and bring to a boil; simmer the fruit until it is falling-apart tender, about 35 minutes. Remove from the heat and purée the fruit and liquid in batches (in the container of a food processor fitted with the steel blade or through a food mill). Return the purée to the rinsed-out casserole and add 1⅓ cups granulated sugar, or more to taste. If you are making apple butter, stir in 1 teaspoon ground cinnamon, ½ teaspoon freshly grated nutmeg, ½ teaspoon ground allspice, and 2 teaspoons finely grated lemon peel; for pear butter, add ½ teaspoon ground allspice, ½ teaspoon ground ginger or 2 teaspoons grated fresh ginger, 2 teaspoons finely grated lemon peel, and 2 tablespoons freshly squeezed lemon juice. Cook the mixture over low heat, stirring frequently, until lightly thickened, about 30 minutes. Cool and store in the refrigerator.

To make fruit butter out of ripe summer fruit (nectarines, peaches, plums, or apricots), peel 3½ pounds of fruit, pit, and cut into pieces. Place the fruit and 1 cup of water in a large nonreactive casserole and cook until tender, about 20 to 25 minutes, then purée with the liquid as outlined above. Return the purée to the casserole and add 1 cup granulated sugar (or more to taste). For nectarine and peach butter, add 1 teaspoon freshly grated nutmeg

and ¼ teaspoon ground cloves; for apricot butter, add 2 teaspoons finely grated orange peel and 2 tablespoons freshly squeezed lemon juice; for plum butter, add 1 teaspoon ground cinnamon and 2 teaspoons finely grated lemon or orange peel. Simmer the butter over low heat for about 20 to 25 minutes, or until lightly thickened. Cool and store in the refrigerator.

## Fruit Compotes

Fruit compotes, made up of small whole fruit (such as apricots and Italian blue plums), or the entire range of dried fruit (peaches, figs, dates, raisins, cherries, mangoes), look like sparkling gems when preserved in a spiced sugar syrup. The fruit is added to the hot prepared syrup and simmered until just tender. Preserved fruit, diced and drained, is ideal for folding through quick bread, fruitcake, and steamed pudding batters, some cookie doughs, softened ice cream, holiday yeast breads, or for layering in baked puddings. Preserved whole fruit, sliced, makes a richly delicious topping for ice cream, pieces of pound cake, or dessert custards, particularly those cooked on top of the stove.

To make a syrup from 2 pounds of fresh fruit, place 1½ cups granulated sugar, 2½ cups water, ½ cup liqueur or brandy, and 2 cinnamon sticks in a nonreactive casserole. Cover and simmer over low heat until the sugar has dissolved completely. Uncover, raise the heat to high and bring to a boil; boil for 3 minutes. In the meantime, prick each piece of fruit several times with a skewer or toothpick to prevent the skin from bursting. Slip the fruit into the syrup, reduce the heat to low, and simmer uncovered until just tender, basting the fruit often, about 4 or 5 minutes. Carefully remove the fruit to a bowl with a slotted spoon and boil the syrup

over high heat for 5 minutes to reduce it. Pick out the cinnamon sticks and add to the fruit. Strain the syrup, cool, and pour over the fruit. Refrigerate the cooled fruit in a covered container.

For a dried fruit compote, add 1½ pounds of dried fruit to hot syrup prepared with compatible spices, and simmer uncovered for 4 or 5 minutes until barely softened (the fruit will continue to soften in the syrup as it cools). Remove the fruit and spices to a bowl; boil the syrup for 4 or 5 minutes, strain, and pour over the fruit while still hot. Cool the fruit completely, transfer to a container, and refrigerate.

Clusters of fresh kumquats, bound cuttings of holly, or tiny homemade pomanders (made by studding small lady apples with cloves) may be attached to the side of a jar of preserved fruit with a length of raffia, making each gift that much more festive.

# 8

# The
# Fruit Kitchen

*Working with fruit*

*Fresh fruit syrups*

*Scented sugars*

Fruit desserts tasting of pure, fresh ingredients are simple to make and easy on the cook. If you love to prepare sweet things, you'll need to have a good pie and tart crust recipe on hand, and know all about the little extras that make desserts special—like making up a batch of homemade fruit syrup or flavored sugar. Over the years, I've acquired formulas and methods for making these recipe enhancements, and offer them to you in this chapter along with a few time-saving techniques for working with fresh fruit.

*The Fruit Kitchen*

# Working with Fruit

Fresh fruit, whether it is sturdy or fragile, needs to be handled thoughtfully. Any finished dessert will look glamorous and appealing if you follow these simple techniques for preparing whole fruit and berries:

*To peel firm-textured fruit (such as pears and apples),* use a swivel-bladed peeler to remove the peel, following the figure of the fruit. For pears, I find it easy to start at the base, then draw the peeler up to the bottom of the stem (taking with it a panel of peel), always moving gently over the surface of the fruit. For apples, use a small sharp paring knife or swivel-bladed peeler and remove the peel by circling around and around the fruit. To core either fruit, cut in half vertically from stem to base with a stainless-steel knife, them remove the core from both halves with a melon ball scoop; trim off the ends, then cut the fruit into slices or chunks.

*To remove the peel from juicy summer fruit (such as peaches or nectarines),* bring a large pot of water to a boil and slip in two or three pieces of fruit at a time. After about 5 to 10 seconds, remove the fruit with a slotted spoon to a bowl filled with ice water. Peel the peaches using a small sharp paring knife; most times, the nectarine peel can be rubbed off with your fingertips; otherwise lightly peel it off with a sharp paring knife.

*To core whole apples and pears (for dumplings and other preparations),* place the fruit stem side up. With a sharp paring knife, cut out a deep cone-shaped cavity from the middle, taking with it the stem and core. If more of the core remains, use a grapefruit knife to scrape it away. To core a pear and leave the stem intact, cut a thin slice off the bottom of the pear and use a grapefruit knife or thin paring knife to cut out the core from the bottom end of the pear.

*Fruit Desserts*

*To prepare berries for use in pie fillings, fruit salads, gratins, cobblers, ice creams, and puddings,* dump the berries into a large colander or onto a platter. Pick out any small twigs, leaves, or thin stems. Rinse the berries quickly under a spray of cool water and drain them thoroughly on sheets of paper towel. Strawberries should be hulled *after* they are rinsed to prevent them from becoming waterlogged.

*To remove the peel from oranges and grapefruit,* cut off a ⅓-inch slice from the top or bottom of the fruit. Beginning at that end, remove rounded strips of peel (including the white pith) with a small serrated knife, using a slightly exaggerated sawing motion. Keep the rounded shape of the fruit intact as you trim away the peel.

Alternatively, you can make good use of the orange or grapefruit peel, and still use the fruit for serving, if you remove the peel with a swivel-bladed peeler. Air-dry the peel and store in a screwtop jar for adding to soups, stews, fruit syrups, and the like later on. Rest the fruit on one end and cut away the bitter pith with a serrated knife, following the lines of the fruit. Then section or slice the fruit, as needed.

*The Fruit Kitchen*

# Fresh Fruit Syrups

Syrups made from whole fruit or berries (or a combination of both) enhance fruit desserts in many ways. A half cup of syrup can replace part of the liquid used for poaching fruit such as pears, peaches, nectarines, plums, or figs; drizzles of syrup can be used over scoops of ice cream or slices of pound cake, to sweeten fruit salads, as the base for ice cream, sherbet, or milkshakes; and adding a few tablespoons of syrup can uplift a plain fruit pie filling.

For *Whole Fruit Syrup*, halve, pit, and dice enough fruit (choose from peaches, plums, apricots, nectarines, pears) to measure 4 cups. This will be about 1¾ to 2 pounds of fruit. Carefully trimmed overripe and bruised fruit can be used. (The pits add flavor to the finished syrup and you can add them along with the fruit, if you wish.) Place the fruit (with pits, if using) in a 6- to 8-quart non-reactive casserole, pour in 1¼ cups water, cover, bring to a boil, and cook until the fruit has softened completely, about 25 to 30 minutes. Remove from the heat, uncover, and cool for 5 minutes. Place a stainless-steel sieve over a large bowl and pour in the fruit mixture (do this in batches), pressing down on the solids each time, and discarding them after each batch is completed. Measure the liquid and return to the rinsed-out casserole. Stir in ½ to ¾ cup granulated sugar (depending on the natural sweetness of the fruits) for every cup of liquid. Cover the casserole and cook the mixture over very low heat until the sugar dissolves completely. Uncover, raise the heat to moderately high, and boil for 5 minutes, or until syrupy. Funnel the liquid into clean, dry bottles, cool completely, cap tightly, and refrigerate.

For *Berry Syrup*, pick over 4 cups berries (choose from blueberries, huckleberries, strawberries, red raspberries, black raspberries, red cherries, or sour "pie" cherries, or a combination of berries);

pit the cherries. Place the berries in a 6- to 8-quart nonreactive casserole, pour in 1 cup water, cover, and bring to a boil. Reduce the heat so that the contents of the casserole simmer steadily for 20 to 25 minutes, or until the berries have cooked down to mush. Remove from the heat. Pour the berry mixture, in batches, into a stainless-steel sieve set over a large measuring cup; press down lightly on the solids to extract the juice without actually pressing the berry mixture through the sieve. Measure the liquid and pour into the rinsed-out casserole. For every cup of liquid add ½ to ¾ cup granulated sugar, depending on the tartness of the berries and your sweet tooth. Cover the casserole and cook over low heat until the sugar dissolves completely, uncover, bring to a boil over moderately high heat, and boil for 3 to 5 minutes, or until syrupy. Fill clean, dry bottles with the syrup, cool completely, cover, and refrigerate.

## A range of syrups

Spring and summer fruit yields a tempting array of syrups. Adding aromatic citrus peel or spices further develops the flavor of the fruit. Strips of orange or lemon peel or whole cinnamon sticks, allspice berries, and cloves may be cooked along with the fruit and water. I always manage to put up bottles of one or more of the following syrups, then bestow them on lucky friends during the winter holiday season. To make any of these syrups, use the amount of liquid and sugar specified for Whole Fruit Syrup or Berry Syrup (above), and proceed as instructed in those recipes.

*Three-Berry Syrup* Measure 4 cups of mixed blueberries, red raspberries, and blackberries.

*Lemon-Peach Syrup* Add 2 tablespoons freshly squeezed lemon juice and 6 strips of lemon peel to 4 cups of diced peaches.

*The Fruit Kitchen*

*Cinnamon-Nectarine Syrup* Add 1 tablespoon freshly squeezed lemon juice, 1 cinnamon stick, and 6 strips of lemon peel to 4 cups of diced nectarines.

*Dark Berry Syrup* Measure 4 cups of mixed blueberries, black raspberries, and blackberries.

*Rum-Plum Syrup* Add 3 tablespoons light or dark rum and 6 whole allspice berries to 4 cups of diced red plums.

*Spiced Apricot Syrup* Add 1 cinnamon stick, 3 whole cloves, 4 whole allspice berries, and ¼ teaspoon freshly grated nutmeg to 4 cups of diced apricots.

*Strawberry-Rhubarb Syrup* Measure 4 cups of mixed hulled strawberries and trimmed, sliced rhubarb.

*Cherry-Vanilla Syrup* Add 1 small whole vanilla bean, split down the center to expose the tiny seeds, to 4 cups of pitted sweet red cherries.

# Scented Sugars

Citrus- or vanilla-bean-flavored sugars, made up in batches and stored in a cool pantry, add a subtle and intriguing taste to many fruit desserts. The sweeteners are delightful used in custard mixtures that form the base for bread pudding, ice cream, or dessert sauces, in a boiled sugar solution used for poaching whole fruit, or in a buttery cake batter. Store these sugars, tightly covered, in a cool pantry.

*Vanilla-Scented Sugar* Pour 3 pounds plain granulated sugar, superfine sugar (also known as "bar" sugar), or confectioners' sugar into a large glass jar. Slit 3 plump vanilla beans and bury them in the sugar. Cover the jar tightly and store at a cool room temperature for 7 to 10 days before using. To use, dip out the sugar, pushing aside the vanilla beans. Over time, vanilla-scented sugar tends to clump here and there; simply break up the soft lumps with the back of a spoon or your fingertips, then measure the sugar.

*Orange-, Tangerine-, or Lemon-Scented Sugar* Using a swivel-bladed peeler, remove 15 strips of orange, tangerine, or lemon peel, taking away as little white pith as possible. Place the lengths of peel on a sheet of wax paper and let stand for 24 hours, or until leathery, turning them once or twice during that time. Pour 3 cups of plain granulated sugar, superfine sugar (also known as "bar" sugar), or confectioners' sugar into a large glass jar. Bury the pieces of dried peel in the sugar, cover tightly, and store at cool room temperature for 2 weeks. After 2 weeks, remove and discard the peel.

# Index

Dried fruit *(cont.)*
  ginger-baked, 139
  mélange of, with cinnamon crème
     fraîche, 14–15
Dumplings
  apple, 64–65
  pear, 65

Empanadas, giant peach, 60–61

Figs, dried
  -applesauce, 24
  in bourbon-vanilla syrup, 19
  ice cream, 147
  maple-baked apples with, 137
Figs, fresh
  in bourbon-vanilla syrup, 18
  clafouti, 87
  in orange juice, 19
Flaky pie crust, 31–35
Floats, lemon, 156–57
Foldover, pear, 62–63
Fool
  apple, 96
  apricot, 96
  blackberry, 96
  peach, 96
  raspberry, 95
  strawberry, 96
Fresh fig clafouti, 87
Fresh fruit tart, 56–58
Frozen mousse
  apricot, 99
  mango, 99
  nectarine, 99
  peach, 98–99
  pear, 99
Fruit, dried. *See also specific dried*
     *fruits*
  and applesauce, 23–24
  clafouti, 84–85
  compotes, 163–64
Fruit, fresh. *See also specific fruits*
  and applesauce, 23–24
  butters, 162–63
  compotes, 163–64

Fruit, fresh *(cont.)*
  medley, summer, with meringues,
     8–9
  preparation tips, 168–69
  tart, 56–58
Fruit salad: summer fruit medley with
     meringues, 8–9

Giant peach empanadas, 60–61
Ginger-baked dried fruit, 139
Gingered pear crisp, 118–19
Ginger-lime syrup, melon compote in,
     10–11
Glaze
  apricot, 56–58
  red currant jelly, 57–58
Glazed orange and grapefruit wedges,
     141
Glazed orange slices, orange-rum
     butter cake with, 46–47
Grapefruit
  and orange compote, 11
  preparation tips, 169
  wedges, glazed orange and, 141

Huckleberry ice cream, 147

Ice
  apple, 151
  lemon, 151
  orange, 150
  peach, 151
  pineapple, 150
Ice cream
  apple, 148–49
  blueberry, 147
  cherry-vanilla, 149
  dried fig, 147
  huckleberry, 147
  nectarine, 147
  peach, 146
  prune-Armagnac, 147
  sodas
    peach, 153
    raspberry cream, 154–55
  strawberry, 147

*Index*

[177]

*Index*

*Index*